Lachmi Bai Rani of Jhansi

Lachmi Bai Rani of Jhansi

the Jeanne D'Arc of India

Michael White

GYAN

Published by

GYAN

Gyan Publishing House
5, Ansari Road
Daryaganj, New Delhi-110002
Phone: 011-47034999, 9811692060
E-mail: books@gyanbooks.com

Distribution Network
gyanbooks.com
India, USA, Canada, UK, Australia, France

ISBN : 978-81-212-9739-4 (PB)
First Published, 1901

2nd Impression 2023

Printed at: Gyan Press, Delhi.

Lachmi Bai Rani of Jhansi
Author: *Michael White*

LACHMI BAI

"Lachmi Bai! Lachmi Bai! Rani of Jhansi!" they cried.—Page 31.

Lachmi Bai

Rani of Jhansi

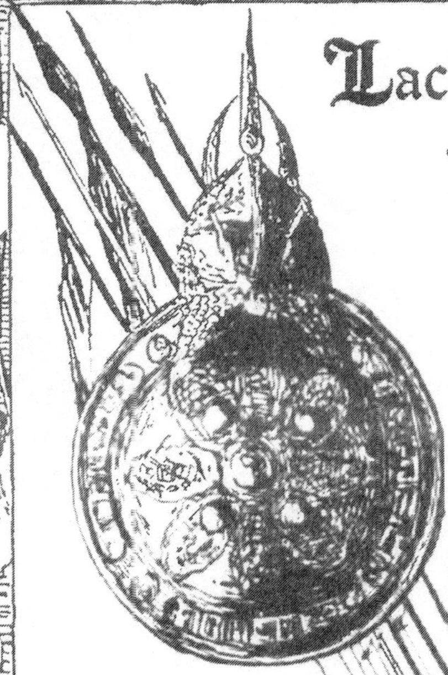

The Jeanne D'Arc of India

By

Michael White

1901

To
my wife

The RANI *of* JHANSI

"Being young, vigorous, and not afraid to show herself to the multitude, she gained a great influence over the hearts of the people. It was this influence, this force of character, added to a splendid and inspiring courage, that enabled her to offer a desperate resistance to the British. . . . Whatever her faults in British eyes may have been, her countrymen will ever believe that she was driven by ill-treatment into rebellion; that her cause was a righteous cause. To them she will always be a heroine."

KAYE AND MALLESON,
"*History of the Indian Mutiny.*"

LACHMI BAI

Within no peerless Taj Mahal her body lies,
No gilded dome, nor fairy minarets against the azure skies,
Proclaim the place, where she, called by her foes, the "bravest and the best,"
Was laid by reverential hands to her victorious rest:
But in the eternal sanctuary of her race,
The holy river, holy Mother Ganges, that coveted embrace,
Doth hold her ashes, and for a monument to her name,
Sufficeth it, that in the people's hearts, her fame,
Doth shine immortal. For she was deeply loved, this Queen,
The beauteous, valiant Rani, India's great heroine.

CONTENTS

LIST OF ILLUSTRATIONS

LACHMI BAI

Chapter I

BEFORE THE STORM

IT was a day of angry, torrid heat. The June sun of Central India blazed fiercely upon an uneven plain, upon a river winding to the northward, a lake bordered by trees, and upon the walled city of Jhansi with its rock fortress rising precipitously to guard the western front. Beneath the south wall, amid groves of acacia, whose parched and dust-coated limbs seemed to implore a speedy descent of the rains then due, were discernible the white domes of temples and tombs. A little further away, surrounded by gardens, were situated the bungalows of the Foreign residents, the cantonments of their troops, and the Star Fort containing their treasure and arms.

The hour of noon approached. Over all a reposeful silence reigned. Everyone had sought the shelter of cool halls and darkened chambers. In the fort and cantonments the soldiers had been dismissed from their duties; on the roads leading to the city there was little traffic; within the gates the bazaars were deserted; not a dog even ventured upon the blistering stones of the palace courtyard. Only in the shadow of a pillar near the main entrance to that turreted structure, a blind beggar sat, every now and then raising his monotonous cry for pity and alms.

Externally, an indefinite era of peace seemed to have settled upon Jhansi. Except for the periodical anxiety concerning the rains, there appeared to be no disquieting feature disturbing its outward calm. Yet for months past in that year of 1857 a token,[1] a warning of some great impending occurrence had gone forth through the land; from whence proceeding few men knew, to what purpose the masses did not comprehend, though they watched. With indifference as to what it might portend, the Foreigners had also observed the sign.

But in one place in Jhansi that day there was no rest at the noontide hour. It was in the palace of the disinherited Rani, or Princess of the state. There, an atmosphere of suspense, an air laden with that mysterious foreboding that some mighty event was about to take place, permeated every apartment, the halls, courts, and corridors. The very walls seemed to live with sinister animation. Men, many of them with arms displayed openly, moved stealthily back and forth from room to room, gathering in groups to discuss some weighty topic with hushed accents. Even the women servants appeared to have caught the infection of the hour, pausing to glean snatches of the men's conversation, and passing on with significant looks.

[1] The *chupaty*, or cake of unleavened bread, that circulated in a mysterious manner previous to the outbreak of the Indian Rebellion.

BEFORE THE STORM

In a small enclosed garden of the palace, where palms, bright-leaved crotons, and fragrant blossoms, afforded a refreshing retreat from the atmospherical furnace without, a man and woman paced side by side in earnest discourse. The man was tall, bronze-visaged, and of martial bearing; the woman slender in form, graceful in carriage, and beautiful in so far as one might gather from features partly concealed by a fold of her embroidered *chuddah.* The former was a Mohammedan noble, Ahmad Khan; the latter, Lachmi Bai, the disinherited Rani of Jhansi.

At a turn in their walk the Princess turned to confront her companion.

"You say, my Lord," she spoke quickly, "that Bahadur Shah once more reigns supreme in Delhi; that the troops at Aligurth have marched out to join his standard; that Bareli has fallen into the hands of Khan Bahadur Khan; and yet there is no news from Bithur. When, in Heaven's name, is Dundhu Panth, the Peshwa, going to send us the signal to rise in Jhansi? For a month past my people have impatiently strained on the leash, awaiting my word to rush forth and drive the Foreigners from the State. I cannot—nay I cannot hold them in hand much longer. God knows, they have their own wrongs as well as mine to redress."

Ahmad raised a hand restrainingly.

"Patience! Patience! my Lady Rani," he exclaimed. "In a little, to-day, to-morrow, surely the Peshwa's messenger will arrive. Restraint will be for the best in the end. The arm of your people will strike all the harder; their onset will be the more irresistible."

"Aye, truly," she replied, "but you forget, O Ahmad, that the Foreigners will not sleep forever. The news from Delhi must have reached their ears. A single traitor might cause them to awake, defeating all our plans. I fear that the blow upon which we have staked so much, may yet fall without cleaving to the heart."

A Native officer in Foreign uniform entered the garden. He halted and saluted.

The Rani and her companion turned quickly toward him with expressions of sudden alarm.

The officer advanced to deliver a message.

"Your Highness," he began, addressing the Rani. "The Commissioner and Captain Sahibs will shortly arrive at the palace to seek an audience. I have been sent forward to acquaint you of their visit."

The Rani stepped close to the officer and scrutinized his features. Then she grasped him tightly by the sleeve of his jacket.

"Thou art the Jamadar Golab Das"? she interrogated.

"As thou sayest, noble Rani."

"Tell me, O Golab," she besought anxiously. "Have they heard? Have the eyes of the Foreigners been opened? Hath a traitor whispered in their ears"?

"They sleep on, all thy people are faithful," the officer returned significantly.

A sigh of relief escaped the Rani's lips.

"It is well," she exclaimed. "Then I will see the Foreign Sahibs. Go, carry them that message."

The officer again saluted and left her presence.

As if a sudden inspiration had gained possession of the Rani's mind, she turned to Ahmad and spoke authoritatively.

"It is my will to see the Foreign Sahibs alone in the *Darbar* hall."

He made a gesture as if about to protest against her purpose.

"Nay," she continued, "Nay, good Ahmad. It is the best plan. If they see me unattended they will be less suspicious. Go, order everyone to hide from view. Let not a face be seen or a voice heard. Let these walls be as silent as a tomb—aye even as the tomb that these Foreigners have built about my life, depriving me of what was justly mine. The palace sleeps, they will say. This woman can do no harm."

She gracefully recognized the Mohammedan noble's bow, signifying his compliance to her order, and moved quickly to a door leading to her private apartments.

At the southern gate of the city, the two Foreign Sahibs, attended by a Native orderly, were met by Golab Das, bearing the Rani's reply.

"Well Jamadar," said the military officer, "What does the Rani say? Did you see her personally"?

"I saw the Princess, your Excellency," returned the Jamadar. "She bade me say that she waits to learn the pleasure of your will."

"Tell me, Jamadar," continued the officer. "Was there any sign of uneasiness about the palace? People gathering, or additions being made to the Rani's bodyguard"?

"My eyes beheld no such gathering of people," returned the Jamadar laconically. "The Rani's servants are resting from the heat."

The officer ordered his subordinate to return to the cantonments. As they moved forward he turned a look of satisfaction toward his companion.

"Well Hawksley," said he. "I doubt after all if we shall have the fun yet of cutting our way through a mass of fanatics."

The Commissioner's face maintained a thoughtful expression.

"I did not anticipate that we would," he returned.

"Yes, but you are as full of gloomy forebodings as any old fortune teller," asserted the other.

"Oh! not at all," exclaimed the Commissioner, "only I think the situation more serious than the rest of us are inclined to regard it."

"What in Jhansi"?

"Yes, in Jhansi. Now look here, Vane," continued the Commissioner gravely. "Let us see how we stand. There is no doubt something horrible has taken place in Delhi."

"Rumors only," interposed the other, "and even then an isolated case. That old rascal, Bahadur Shah, will soon be brought to his senses, and punished drop for drop of our blood."

"I hope so," remarked the Commissioner. "But this morning I heard that the troops at Bareli had revolted and seized the place."

"A band of marauders," added the soldier lightly. They will be hanged when caught, every one of them. For my part, I fail to perceive how these scattered outbreaks are likely to affect us in Jhansi."

"Yes, indirectly they may," the Commissioner persisted. "Now look here, Vane. Think a moment seriously, if you can do such a thing. Here we are a paltry hundred and fifty odd Europeans in the heart of India, far removed from the least chance of assistance."

"We shall not need any," remarked the soldier emphatically. "If the people hereabout should create any disturbance, my men will soon deal with them. They have sworn to a unit that they will stand by their salt oath of allegiance. I have implicit confidence in them."

"Granted! Granted that what you assert may be true," rejoined the Commissioner, "but to my mind the element of danger here lies in another direction."

"Where pray"? demanded the other dubiously.

They had passed the gate and were traversing the almost deserted bazaars.

"Where pray"? he asked again, glancing along a row of empty stalls. "I confess, I fail to note any sign of it."

"Perhaps not," rejoined the Commissioner, "but it is in evidence nevertheless. I refer to the Rani."

"What, to that girl, the Rani," the officer exclaimed.

" Nonsense! What mischief can she do. Her talons have been well pared for any evil that she might design."

" My dear Vane," said the Commissioner sagely. " Never underestimate the power and resources of a woman, if she nourishes a grievance."

" A grievance? "

" Yes, frankly, though unofficially, I consider that she has a grievance—even a just one against us. Now what is her position? First, we took from her the estate of her affianced husband, that by her law she was clearly entitled to hold."

" But transferred, I thought, according to the provisions of a treaty made with the late Raja."

" True, but still she was none the less a heavy loser by it. Well then, by way of recompense for this, what did we do? We gave her a paltry $30,000 a year."

" A devilish good allowance, I call it," flippantly interposed Vane. " I only wish I had $30,000 a year, and the Rani or the deuce might do what they pleased with Jhansi. Dear old Pall Mall would soon see me on the double."

The Commissioner refused to notice his companion's light humor.

" Out of that allowance," he proceeded, " small enough in all conscience for one in her position, we insisted on deducting a sinking fund to pay the late Raja's debts."

Vane struck his boot a smart rap with the end of his whip.

" Oh, hang it! " he exclaimed. " That was bad. It's

shocking enough to be obliged to meet one's own *i. o. u.'s;* but to settle up for another fellow is monstrous. My sympathy there is with the Rani, though it wasn't our fault, you know."

"Yes, I thought that would appeal to you," remarked the Commissioner dryly, "but if I am not mistaken that matter of killing cows, in spite of her protests, has enraged her more than the loss of either the Jhansi throne or the revenue. That, was an unnecessary insult to her religious sensibilities. Now what I maintain is this, if she has been waiting for a favorable opportunity to strike a blow for what she may regard as her lost position and injured feelings, the present is as good a one as she is likely to be afforded. Her influence with the people is, I am convinced, a quantity worth taking into account."

Vane yawned with the heat and the little interest he felt in both the subject and the visit. He was satisfied that the Commissioner's fears were groundless, that there was not the slightest danger of an outbreak in Jhansi, and only with difficulty had he been persuaded to accompany his colleague to the Rani's palace.

"In any case, suppose there is something in your idea," he asked, "what can she do?"

"That is exactly what we are going to try and discover," returned the Commissioner firmly.

They had arrived before the main entrance to the palace. They dismounted and handed the reins of their horses to the native orderly.

Vane glanced contemptuously at an obsequious aged servant who had come forth to receive them, and round upon the drowsy appearance of the buildings.

"Conspiracy! Uprising of the people! Nonsense"! he ejaculated. "Hawksley's imagination has gone wandering. I'd wager six months' pay the girl is trembling at the bare idea of our visit."

As the request for an audience had been made upon the spur of the moment, the Commissioner regarded it as a favorable sign that the Rani consented to receive them without delay.

They were ushered through an inner courtyard surrounded by cloisters, in the shade of which a few Natives awoke to salute the Foreign Sahibs as they passed. Thence through dark halls and ante-chambers, in which the echo of their footsteps alone broke the profound silence that had descended on the palace. At last they crossed the threshold of the *Darbar* hall.

At the further end of the noble chamber, where for centuries it had been the custom of the Princes of Jhansi to dispense justice, she, from whom justice had been withheld, stood to receive her visitors. In the sight of the two officers as they gazed down a nave of pillars supporting the ornately decorated roof, she appeared as the statue of some divinity in the far perspective of an ancient temple—a youthful, white robed, graceful figure, brought into strong relief by a dark background of gold embroidered arras.

As if to emphasize the powerless condition to which

she had been reduced, the Rani was attended by a single waiting woman, who remained throughout the interview a few paces in her rear, motionless and apparently unobservant.

The officers advanced to within a few paces of her position and saluted her respectfully.

With a slight inclination of her head, she acknowledged their greeting and waited to learn the nature of their errand.

The Commissioner had anticipated that the Rani would have hastily surrounded herself with numerous retainers to impress him with a semblance of her power. He realized that a hundred splendidly attired courtiers could not have added a shade of prestige to this girl, who stood alone.

It was not only the majestic pose, nor the beautiful contour of her face, crowned by a mass of dark hair, ornamented with a chaplet of pearls, that quickly confirmed the Commissioner's previous impression that Lachmi Bai, Rani of Jhansi, was far removed from the generally accepted type of her countrywomen. But there was a strength of character emphasized in every line of her distinctly Aryan features, a force of will, a mystical power in every flash of her lustrous eyes, in every movement, in every word, however gently spoken, warning him at the outset that he had to deal with no shrinking, simple, *zanana* maiden.

He had come prepared to assume a firm, if necessary a dictatorial attitude; but now in her presence he found himself slowly paving the way by conventional compliments.

Her silence at last compelled him to come to the point. "Your Highness," he began, "will doubtless have heard of the disturbances that have broken out in several districts of the Northwest Provinces."

"Some reports have reached my ears," she replied, with apparent indifference, "but I give to them little credence."

"I am afraid," resumed the Commissioner gravely, "that there is only too much reason to believe their authenticity. I have, therefore, sought this audience with your Highness to request that in the event of any threatened outbreak in Jhansi, you will use your influence to preserve peace. I need not add that by so doing, by demonstrating at such a crisis that your sympathy is with the British Government, you will be rendering a service to the latter that I, personally, will guarantee shall not be overlooked."

The representative of the power that had deprived her of her possessions stood before her as a supplicant for her good will.

A nature less subtle, less under such admirable control, might at the moment have been over tempted to cast prudence to the winds, and in an outburst of long gathering passion jeopardize the complete success of her plans by summoning her retainers to seize prematurely the persons of the British officers. But trained in adversity, that best of schools to curb her real feelings, by not a sign did she betray, that for months past she had been preparing for the hour when the fate of Jhansi should rest in the palm of her hand; nor the infallible knowledge she possessed, that every man in the city, aye even every woman and child, together with the whole body of native troops within the British cantonments, awaited her signal to rise in revolt.

In a voice, in which only the faintest note of irony was mingled with surprise, she answered quietly.

"Surely the Foreign Sahib sets too great store upon my ability to assist him. What have I," she continued, raising the tone slightly, and extending a hand so that the gold bangles on her wrist jingled musically. "What influence hath Lachmi Bai with the people to control their actions? If they should rebel, has not the Sahib soldiers and guns to enforce his will; I, but a few poor servants to protect my person. No," she concluded, letting her hand fall again to her side, "the Sahib knows well I have no power, no authority in Jhansi."

The Commissioner twirled his moustache musingly. He knew that without doubt she had stated the literal truth; but he was now more firmly convinced than ever, that behind the dark eyes which so unflinchingly returned his gaze, there lay a power for good or evil in a possible emergency, that it would be suicidal to ignore.

Gravely he resumed the subject.

"It would be a poor compliment," he said, "to the esteem in which it is well known your Highness is held by the people, to place your influence at so low a value.

Should an uprising take place in Jhansi, you could do much to preserve law and order."

For a few moments neither spoke. Each regarded the other as if endeavoring to find a vulnerable point in the contest of diplomacy, when the Rani skilfully turned the subject to her own advantage. She was anxious to discover if any suspicion of her plans had been engendered in the minds of the Foreigners, and how far they depended for their safety upon the fidelity of their native troops, already won over to her cause. She therefore replied by another question.

"But have you any reason to think that the peace will be broken in Jhansi"?

"At present, I have not," the Commissioner replied, after a short period of reflection.

"And even in that event you can surely rely upon the loyalty of your native troops"? she suggested with apparent absence of motive.

"Yes, I believe so," he affirmed decisively. "Certainly they will remain true to their salt."

"Then why come to me," she asked, "to seek assistance for which you are likely to have so little need"?

The Commissioner realized that argumentatively, his position was no longer tenable. So he determined to revert to his original purpose and make a firm demand upon the evasive young Princess.

"Nevertheless," he replied sternly. "It is my duty to inform you, that the British Government will hold you responsible for any outbreak among the people."

The Rani raised her eyebrows slightly, as she retorted in a rising tone of protest.

"Surely the Commissioner Sahib does not remember the position in which his Government has placed me. He forgets that it not only deprived me of my inheritance of the throne of Jhansi, but of my affianced husband's personal estates, and even compelled me out of the pittance of an allowance provided for my support to pay his debts. Thus, often have the poor in vain cried to me to alleviate their distress, daily are Brahmans turned from my gates unfed. I cannot help them. For the reason that you have deprived me of the means wherewith even to influence the actions of a beggar, I cannot assist you. I do not see, nay, I do not understand how I can be held responsible for the public peace. As well might you extract the teeth of a watch dog and expect it to guard your treasure safely. Does your Government also hold me responsible for the loyalty of your troops"? she concluded, with a note of scorn.

"No," he returned with emphasis, "but it will undoubtedly look to your Highness to act in the event of an outbreak, as I have suggested."

The ultimatum had been delivered.

The two officers bowed to the Rani and retraced their steps to the end of the hall. On the threshold Vane paused for a moment. He glanced over his shoulder and met the gaze of the Rani still fixed upon them. With her hands folded she had remained in the same position; but there was an unmistakable expression of scornful triumph on her face, carrying swift conviction to his mind, that their mission had failed, that this mere girl had routed their arguments and baffled their diplomacy.

As they passed down the steps, he linked his arm in that of his companion. He spoke in an undertone, with no vestige of his flippant humor remaining.

"I say, Hawksley. I say, old fellow. D'you know, I thing the Rani is a devilish clever girl. We didn't get much out of her, did we"?

The Commissioner eyed his companion seriously.

"Yes," he acquiesced. "For my part, Vane, I believe it would have been better for all of us if we had arrived at that conclusion before."

They had scarcely disappeared from the hall, when white figures seemed to emerge from the very walls.

The Rani waved them back with a warning gesture.

"Go," she enjoined her attendant. "Go, Rati, and see if the Foreigners have left the court."

In a few minutes the girl returned with the information that the Foreign Sahibs had mounted their horses.

The Rani raised her arms above her head and cried aloud as she gave full vent to her suppressed emotion.

"Fools! Fools all! Of what do they think I am made. Am I clay to be moulded into any form, a pitcher with which to draw water for them when thirsty? Ah! By the great God of Gods, I swear that before another sun has set, they shall find that the will, if not the form of Lachmi Bai is fashioned out of steel."

Quickly she was surrounded by an eager throng, clamoring for news of the audience.

"What said the Foreign Sahibs, O Rani"? they besought her. "Tell us, O Queen, what said they"?

She waved them from her gently.

"It is enough," she cried, "that still hearing no sound but the call to plunder, they are deaf to the mighty whisper passed down from palace to hovel, and on from city to jungle, that the hour for India is at hand."

Chapter II

THE HOUR AT HAND

IN a shaded room of the palace, the Rani had cast herself upon a low divan to obtain a short period of rest. The rugs of intricate patterns, embroidered hangings, curiously carved and inlaid screens, tables, and taborets, gave to the apartment an atmosphere more of richness, than comfort from the Occidental point of view. She watched reflectively the actions of her waiting woman in placing a smoking paraphernalia at her side.

"Strange, how strange," she murmured, "are the ways of these Foreigners. After all the wrongs they have visited upon me, the insults I have suffered at their hands; they boldly come and demand my influence to maintain such iniquities. They expect, forsooth, that if the door of my prison is opened, I will close it again upon myself. Surely they must think I possess less reason than a creature bereft of its senses. I—I cannot understand them."

She turned her head to notice a stout, little man, *salaaming* profoundly.

"Well, good Bipin," she exclaimed. "What matter of supreme weight and urgency is it now? Hath an evil minded fox crossed thy path on thy way to the temple, or a crow dropped a tail feather with sinister intent upon thy turban"?

"Protector of thy People," replied Bipin, "your Extraordinary Greatness will be pleased to know, that the illustrious Raja, Sivapuri Prasad Singh, an emissary from the Peshwa, awaits your Highness's command to enter."

The Rani rose to her feet instantly, manifesting intense emotion in her voice and actions, as she cried:

"The Peshwa's messenger at last. Go, good Bipin, bring him to me immediately. There is no one I long to see more than this same emissary from the Peshwa."

She had scarcely spoken when Bipin ushered into the room a Hindu noble of gallant mien, whose attire bore traces of hasty travel through jungle by-paths. He strode hurriedly forward and bowing before the Rani, glanced round with suspicion.

The Rani waved her male servitor from the room.

"Speak, noble sir," she urged reassuringly. "The walls are deaf as well as dumb. Ah, *Mahadeva!* How anxiously we have awaited thy coming."

"Good news, My Lady Rani," he replied, in an undertone. "The torch has been ignited. To-morrow Dundhu Panth proclaims himself Peshwa, and Cawnpore will fall into his hands. Strike now, for if Jhansi is won, other states, that waver, will follow suit. Such is the Peshwa's command."

"Welcome, most welcome, noble Raja," she cried, in a transport of joyful emotion. She extended her hands in greeting. "Welcome to the palace of the no longer unfortunate Rani of Jhansi."

He took the jeweled fingers of one of her hands in

his and bowing low placed them to his forehead. Then he drew himself up and gazed with sudden admiration at the superb form, the beautiful features of the high caste Princess.

In a moment he resumed the conversation, still in a tone of caution.

"Are all thy plans complete, fair Lady"?

"Aye, even over complete, I had feared," she answered. "The hidden guns in the fortress have been disinterred, my retainers armed, guards posted on the highways to prevent the escape of the Foreigners, when the signal is given. All people in Jhansi wait impatiently upon my word."

"It is well," he exclaimed, approvingly. "But how about the Mohammedans? Can they be depended upon"?

"Ahmad Khan moves them at the raising of his hand."

"Aye, but of Ahmad Khan. At the raising of whose hand doth he obey without question?"

The Rani slowly raised her hand and held it outstretched before her.

A dart of racial jealousy pierced the Hindu noble's breast.

"Ah!" he exclaimed. "It is perhaps well thus, for the moment."

The Rani's arm fell lightly to her side.

"It is well for all time, so long as we are united," she returned, with significant emphasis.

Prasad moved a step nearer and spoke almost in a whisper.

"What of the Foreigners? Do they suspect a rising"?

"They are in doubt, but rely implicitly upon the fidelity of their Native troops."

"Will their Native troops join us"?

"Every man among them."

"Are you certain"?

"As certain as that the wolf will hunt with his kind."

Prasad paused thoughtfully before putting another question.

"If we succeed what is to be done with the Foreigners"?

"Ahmad has my order to secure them as prisoners. We will hold them as hostages or send them out of the state.

Prasad took the Rani's hand in his and pressed it gently. Already he was a slave to her will. Henceforth the form of Lachmi Bai filled his soul with one aim above all others.

"Ah, my Lord," she cried, turning a radiant countenance toward him. "How long hath my heart pined for this hour—the hour when the scepter which was snatched from my grasp shall be placed in my hand; and the law of the Foreigner be no longer obeyed in Jhansi."

"Surely it is thy right, noble Rani," he replied. "When then can the signal be given?"

"Now, to-night, to-morrow, at any time."

"Then make certain that all is ready to-night, and let the signal be given for to-morrow."

The Rani beckoned her waiting woman to her side.

"Go," said she. "Go swiftly, let it be known that to-morrow at noon, the tigress will break down the bars of her cage."

Chapter III

BY THE VOICE OF THE PEOPLE

JHANSI had fallen. At the revolt of their troops the Foreigners were taken completely by surprise. They hastily retreated to the Star Fort where, after a valorous defense for three days, lack of food and ammunition compelled them to surrender. They were obliged to seek terms of Ahmad Khan who was conducting the siege.

If they evacuated the fort would they be permitted to leave the state unmolested? was the request made under a flag of truce.

In response, Ahmad solemnly swore upon the holy Koran that if the Foreigners would open the gates no harm should befall them.

But the oath of the Mohammedan was not regarded as sufficiently binding. The Foreigners required a further assurance of safety from the Rani.

In her name Ahmad reiterated his vow of protection. This was all the hope of security they could possibly look for in their desperate situation. The Rani had ever been regarded as an upright woman. Upon the faith of her word they opened the gates and laid down their arms. Then under Ahmad's direction they marched out to a field nearby,—a pitiful, defenseless band, of men, women, and children.

The sun never shone upon a more brutal tragedy.

Beside a clump of trees all were ruthlessly butchered. Their honor alone was spared. Without a plea for mercy, without a cry of anguish, these heroes met a cruel fate, that might have been averted by a less exacting government.

Ahmad Khan was elated almost to a condition of intoxication by this final successful act of the revolt. He was now prompted to strike another immediate blow to gratify a long secretly nourished ambition. While outwardly he had professed intense devotion to the Rani's cause, in his heart, he aspired to seat himself on the throne of the Rajas of Jhansi. As to the Rani, he purposed that her rule should be encompassed by the walls of a luxurious *harem.*

At the head of a crime-frenzied Mohammedan band, bearing upon the points of their bayonets ghastly trophies of the recent massacre, he set forth on a triumphant progress to the palace.

To secure his object, he instructed his followers to overawe the Hindu population, devoted to the Rani's cause, by fierce gestures and loud shouts in his honor.

He entered the gate set in the massive stone wall; and waved his sword aloft crying—

"The Faith. The holy Faith. Success to the Faith of Mohammed."

His soldiers pressed closely upon the flanks of his horse. They brandished their weapons and struck dismay into the hearts of the Hindu guard, by adding exultingly to their distinctive shout of victory—

"And may Ahmad Khan, the Servant of God, long reign in Jhansi."

Onward the mob swept through the city, again and again vociferously proclaiming Ahmad Khan, Raja of Jhansi. The joy of the Hindus over their deliverance from Foreign rule gave place to alarm. They watched with misgiving a second *coup d' etat* on the part of their hereditary enemies, and began to wonder whether they would not fare worse under the rule of a follower of Mohammed, than they had done under that of the Foreigner.

In her palace the Rani anxiously awaited news of the surrender. Through Ahmad she had given the assurance that the Foreigners' lives would be spared. This course she had strenuously urged upon her lieutenant. Apart from her womanly repugnance to ruthless slaughter, she clearly perceived the advantage she would gain by holding them as prisoners to exchange for the recognition of her right to the throne of Jhansi. To kill the innocent, the already defeated, did not occupy a thought in her mind.

The news came swift and ominous. Not only had a tragedy taken place, but her own authority was in danger of usurpation.

The exultant Mohammedan cry rolled forward to the walls of the palace. It penetrated to the Rani's ears at first as a welcome sound; but as it rose in the courtyard bearing aloft the name of Ahmad Khan, a disquieting thought flashed into her brain.

She hurried to the *Darbar* hall, entering at one end, as

Ahmad, surrounded by his officers, crossed the threshold at the other.

The Rani halted and waited. Intuitively she gleaned confirmation of her sudden alarm from their faces.

Ahmad advanced and saluted her with pointed courtesy. He was a tall, powerfully built man, whose swarthy irregular features indicated a mingling of low caste blood. As a whole his face was not unhandsome, though the expression of his mouth and chin denoted cruelty and treachery—the latter, perhaps, an accomplishment rather than a failing to the Oriental mind.

"Greeting, fair Lady," he exclaimed. "Jhansi is won. The Foreigners have surrendered."

She directed a searching glance to read the veiled meaning expressed in his intonation as well as in his manner.

"They have surrendered. Then where are they"? she asked. "Hast thou not brought any of them hither"?

A cruel smile broke upon Ahmad's face as he turned and pointed with the blade of his sword to the open doorway, through which could be caught a glimpse of the surging mob without, uplifting their bloody trophies.

"Aye," he explained, "I have brought some of them here. The rest I have sent to a secure prison."

His gesture was observed by his followers. The shout rose with greater volume than before—

"*Deen! Deen! Futteh. Mohammed.*"

"Success to the Faith of Mohammed."

For a moment the Rani covered her eyes with her

hands, as if to blot out the gruesome spectacle. Then she demanded sternly—

"Why hast thou done this, my Lord? Surely thou hast not killed them all"?

"Aye, all, fair Lady. And why not"? he returned, in plausible accents.

"Because I commanded you to spare their lives if they surrendered," she retorted, passionately.

Ahmad bowed low with feigned contrition.

"But, my Lady Lachmi Bai," he protested, "a higher authority, the Emperor of Delhi, had commanded me to spare none of them. Further his Majesty hath been pleased to place the government of the State of Jhansi in my hands until more settled times."

The two stood for a short period confronting each other in silence. Ahmad with a look of unconcealed triumph on his face, on that of the Rani, anger mingled with defiance.

"So this was his purpose! A plot within a plot revealed."

He strode up to her and with assurance took her by the hand. Then he spoke in a lower voice.

"Ah! Fair Rani. Thou art but a child, a girl fit rather to play with gems than swords and scepters. But fear not, thou shalt rule in Jhansi. Thou knowest well for what I hunger. All that thou longest for, thou shalt possess in return. It is a good bargain, is it not, Beautiful One"?

Her glance swept from his face to the crowd of his

officers standing to his order in the background. She realized that the dominion for which she had so long and patiently striven was about to be seized by another at the moment of its accomplishment. By one, too whose religious principles were repugnant, and whose profession of personal devotion she had but tolerated for reasons of state. She saw the trap into which she had fallen, and from which an immediate counterstroke of diplomacy could alone save her.

Her mind was quick to grasp the situation and suggest a remedy.

With an effort she curbed her resentment and turned a look of approval upon the traitor.

"Aye, thou speakest truly," she replied, in a thoughtful tone. "I am, as thou sayest, but a girl, to whom the reins of government would be of little pleasure. I had longed that the Foreigners be driven forth from Jhansi. Now they are here no more to anger me, why should I not be satisfied? But, O Ahmad," she continued confidentially, "I would speak with thee alone. Send, I pray thee, these people of thine from the palace. I like not their fierce looks and clash of arms."

Ahmad was surprised. He had anticipated a stormy scene with the Rani, and a possible resort to force before she could be brought to submit to his will. Consequently he was gratified to meet with so little resistance to both his political and personal designs. For the moment he failed to remember that the brain which had displayed such masterly craft in plotting the downfall of the Foreigners would be swift to use the same power in frustrating his own project.

In compliance with her desire he faced his officers.

"Go," he commanded. "Return to the cantonments and in my name seize all the possessions of the Foreigners."

When the soldiers had left the hall the Rani drew close to him and spoke in a beguiling voice.

"O my Lord, thou must see how poorly I am attired in honor of so great an event. I would retire for a short space, to adorn my neck with jewels, and my hair with flowers; so that I may appear worthy of the noble Ahmad Khan's approval."

Blinded by vanity, he was flattered and deceived by her cajolery. He stretched forth his arms to enfold her in an embrace.

"Thou shadow of an *houri,*" he exclaimed amorously.

She eluded him by a quick movement.

"In a little," she returned, playfully. "See that thou waitest until I come again to thee. Then shalt thou swear by thy Prophet's beard, that Lachmi Bai hath wit as well as beauty."

"Until death," he replied, "only tarry not too long, Fair One."

She cast toward him an enthralling glance, and passing from the hall, hurried to the inner apartments of the palace.

"Now by Allah"! he reflected, exultingly. "The fortune of Ahmad Khan, the Humble Servant of God, doth rise as the sun in a cloudless heaven."

The Rani's action was swift and silent. She summoned those upon whom she could rely and spoke in urgent accents.

"Go quickly," she commanded to one, "into the bazaars and summon all my people to the courtyard of the palace." To another, "Let my retainers arm themselves and guard every outlet so that no man passes in or forth. Tell Prasad and my officers, that I need their presence on the balcony overlooking the main entrance. Go, with wings on your feet. Hasten, for there is no time to be lost."

She passed into a private chamber and hastily arrayed herself in a magnificent embroidered *sari,* the silken clinging texture of which displayed her form to its perfection of royal beauty. Round her neck she hung ropes of pearls, and in her hair she entwined a wreath of fragrant blossoms. Thus attired she proceeded to the wide balcony overlooking the courtyard.

A throng of people had gathered and crowded about the main entrance. Others were hurrying from the bazaars and side streets at the bidding of the Rani's messengers. With animated countenances, they asked of each other the meaning of the summons.

Behind the domes and turrets of the rock citadel, the sun was sinking toward the horizon. It cast broad shadows over the courtyard, now filling rapidly with a surging, excited, human mass. The Rani was quickly joined by

Prasad and officers faithful to her service. With these in attendance she moved to the edge of the parapet.

Immediately an outburst of enthusiasm rose from the people, gathering in force until a great shout filled the air about the palace.

"Lachmi Bai. Lachmai Bai. Rani of Jhansi," they cried.

She leaned over the parapet and smiled.

Again the cry rose, "Lachmi Bai. Lachmi Bai. Rani of Jhansi."

She raised her hand to enjoin silence. Gradually the tumult ceased.

Then she spoke to them. Her resonant, clear, voice filled the open space. Each word fell musically upon the ears of her audience.

"My people," she began. "At last you have been freed from the rule of the Foreigner. To-day, a great blow has been delivered by you for our independence—a blow that will resound in the most distant provinces of our land. Through your loyalty and courage, the end for which we have so long striven has been attained. To you belongs the spoil, the treasure that has fallen into our hands. It is your reward."

A murmur of applause told that the point had been well received.

"But my people," she proceeded. "You are still encompassed by great peril. The Foreigner is destroyed, but others of his race may return to try and wrest from you, your country. Enemies, too, may rise from within as rapacious and as hateful of your religion. It is necessary that you choose without delay a fearless and capable ruler."

A few voices called on her by name, but she again silenced them.

"As you well know," she continued, "by our law, to me belongs the right of succession to the throne of Jhansi."

"Aye, truly," many cried. "Lachmi Bai. Lachmi Bai. Rani of Jhansi."

"But, my good people, as the noble Raja, Ahmad Khan, hath pointed out, I am but a girl, uninstructed in the wiles of statecraft, unused to the wielding of a sword in dangerous times. A Raja, he declares, must be seated on the throne of Jhansi. Why not then the illustrious Ahmad Khan"?

Spontaneously the cry rose, "For us no stranger, no Mohammedan! We want him not to rule over us. Lachmi Bai. Lachmi Bai. Rani of Jhansi."

"But, good people," she persisted, as if earnestly pleading Ahmad's cause. "Ahmad Khan is a brave soldier. He is"——

Her voice was drowned in an uproar that shook the walls of the palace. Her name alone was borne upward by thousands of unyielding throats.

"Lachmi Bai. Rani of Jhansi. Lachmi Bai. Rani of Jhansi."

She stretched out her arms lovingly toward them. She appealed to them with a captivating smile.

"Would you then have Lachmi Bai for your ruler in Jhansi"?

A great shout rose and confirmed her in her right to the title. The throngs surged back and forth in the endeavor of those furthest away to reach a spot nearer to her person.

"Come to us," they cried. "Come down amid thy people, O Rani."

With a radiant countenance, she passed down the flight of stone steps into the courtyard. Unguarded she moved among the mass of people, stirred to a frenzy of enthusiasm by her presence. Some knelt in her path to touch the hem of her garment, while others waved their weapons aloft, vowing they would defend her to the death.

Darkness fell with the swiftness of the Tropics. She turned to re-enter the palace, and torches flared to light her path. They gave to the scene a weird, majestic splendor—the irregular outlines of the palace overshadowed by the huge black mass of the fortress; the exultant, white robed throng; the stern faces of the soldiers; the girl, whose mysterious being swayed their emotions like the wind playing upon lotus reeds.

In the *Darbar* hall Ahmad Khan impatiently awaited the Rani's return. He was startled by the cries of the populace, and dismayed at the discovery that his egress was blocked. Uneasily he paced back and forth, wondering what these ominous signs betokened. He cursed his imprudence at having dismissed his followers at so critical a moment.

"Tricked, I doubt not," he savagely exclaimed. "But one more fool who loses a crown in exchange for a woman's smile."

The Rani and her officers swept into the hall. Ahmad's hand impulsively grasped the hilt of his sword—a gesture which Prasad imitated by half withdrawing his from its scabbard.

The Hindu noble advanced a few paces, regarding Ahmad's sullen countenance as if willing to accept a challenge.

"Peace, my Lords," the Rani cried authoritatively.

She laid a restraining hand on Prasad's arm.

"Peace. It is my will. This is no hour to broach a feud."

She then fearlessly advanced to Ahmad's side, and addressed him calmly.

"My Lord Raja," said she. "My people will have it that I rule over Jhansi."

She held up her hand to draw his attention to the acclamations which penetrated the innermost recesses of the palace.

"You hear them," she continued. "I espoused your cause to the best of my ability; but, it seems, they will have no other than Lachmi Bai to be their Rani."

"And now," she concluded, addressing all present, "I look to you, Ahmad, Prasad, and all my brave officers to unite for one object, the defense of my throne and Jhansi."

Ahmad glanced round upon the determined faces of the

Rani's loyal supporters, as they vowed to maintain the crown upon her head. He realized that, in turn, he had been outwitted. By a low obeisance he outwardly acknowledged her authority.

"The people are God's," he murmured, "the country is the *Padshah's,* and the *Raj* is the Rani's."

Thus was Lachmi Bai proclaimed Rani of Jhansi.

Chapter IV

A STAR IN THE ASCENDENT

THE Rani's ambition to ascend the throne of Jhansi was achieved. But immediately she beheld difficulties rise on all sides. Everyone in Jhansi seemed to have a claim to urge upon her gratitude. The larger the pecuniary recompense that was supposed to be attached to a place of honor, the more numerous were the applicants. To that of the greatest responsibility, the command of the troops, the Rani was in a dilemma as to whom she would appoint.

From his well known military skill and tried valor, Ahmad Khan might wisely have been selected for the office; but the Rani hesitated to confide to his hands so much power after his recent exhibition of disloyalty.

In the meantime Ahmad had sullenly retired to his house without the city, there to plead sickness as an excuse for failing to respond to her summons to court.

On the other hand, Prasad remained close to her side, hourly transforming the early esteem which the Rani had conceived for him, into a warmer sentiment. He, too, intimated that his aspiration lay toward the chief military prize in the Rani's gift; but thus far she had let it pass ungratified, if not unrecognized. Apart from his untried ability as a commander, she realized that to appoint Prasad, a newcomer to the state, to such a coveted position, would surely stir up a feeling of bitter jealousy in the breasts of a score of Jhansi officers, who might justly claim a prior right to her consideration. These matters increasingly harassèd the Rani's mind.

The morning of a few days after her accession discovered the Rani in the act of formally announcing that event, by letter, to the other princes who had risen in rebellion against the rule of the Foreigners.

Before her, Bipin Dat sat cross-legged upon a mat. He was laboriously endeavoring to indite these missives in what he considered to be correct form.

After a period of effort, he drew the Rani's attention to his latest production.

"This letter, noble Rani," said he, "is to the most illustrious Dhundu Panth, Peshwa of the Marathas."

The Rani signified her willingness to listen, and Bipin proceeded to read in a sonorous voice, emphasizing the repetition of his own name by inflection of tone, and gestures—

By the hand of the Intellectual
Bipin Dat
Secretary to Her Highness, Lachmi Bai,
Rani of Jhansi
To
The most noble, Dhundu Panth,
Peshwa of the Marathas
Greeting

"Be it known to you, O most Illustrious Sir, that by the will of God and the pleasure of the great Rani, the Honorable Bipin Dat ventures to address your Sublimity, for the purpose of disclosing certain information, as follows:

"On the 8th of the month the Foreigners were obliterated from the face of the earth in Jhansi, as if the devil had swept them all off into Hades. Further, on the same day, it pleased the great God to direct His people to seat Her Immortal Highness, Lachmi Bai, upon the throne of the Rajas of Jhansi, which events were witnessed by the observant eye, and recorded by the unerring hand of her faithful and esteemed servant, Bipin Dat.

"Lastly, it hath pleased Her Highness the Rani, to recognize the services of the aforesaid Bipin Dat in these great times, by appointing him her *munshi*.[1] Whereby he has set his hand to this letter on the 12th day of the month, etc.

(Signed) "BIPIN DAT,
"Secretary to the Rani of Jhansi."

Bipin finished his reading with a flourish of the hand and a look upon his solemnly cherubic countenance, that indicated his perfect satisfaction with the composition.

"That, noble Rani," said he, "will in proper form convey to the Peshwa the news of your Highness's accession."

A smile momentarily relieved the Rani's serious expression.

[1] Secretary.

"He will also," she remarked, "be in little doubt as to the identity of the writer. The Peshwa, the Rani, and the Intellectual Bipin Dat. He may wonder if the third is not the most important of the three."

Bipin stroked his chin musingly.

"Dust under thy feet," he replied at last. "That could scarcely be the case, but it has ever been the opinion of the most learned *pundits* that in the work of great writers their personality shines forth as a diamond amid false gems."

"Then Bipin, thou must be a veritable stone of the first water," she replied. "But one thing I gather. You, at any rate, out of a multitude of aspirants for office, appear satisfied with your position."

"Noble Rani," he continued. "Satisfied am I of thy graciousness; but of the precise moment when it will be advisable for me formally to take upon myself the burden of my duties, I am not yet determined."

A look of displeasure crossed the Rani's face.

"How mean you?" she asked. "Have you, too, some petition to make that I will exchange it for one that brings a better revenue?"

"Noble Lady," he replied, "mere wealth holds out little inducement for those of intellectual worth. We, who are writers with inspired thoughts, look for a more imperishable reward; but in all events of importance it is ever well to consult those who read the future and who can discern the most auspicious moment to take an important step."

"Oh!" exclaimed the Rani. "Thou wouldst consult thy friend, the astrologer?"

Bipin bowed.

"Such is my desire, noble Lady."

"Go, then," she cried, "and get thy consultation over quickly, for I need the service of thy pen."

Bipin rose from his sitting posture. He *salaamed* thrice before his mistress and departed with an important air.

In the shadow of the pillar by the main entrance the blind beggar, who appeared to have sat there from the beginning of all time, instinctively recognized Bipin's footsteps. He accosted the secretary with a petition for alms.

"Good clerk," he cried. "Have pity upon the unfortunate."

Bipin halted and faced him with a look of offended dignity.

"Good clerk!" he returned, in scornful accents. "Good clerk! Thou fool. Dost know to whom thou art speaking?"

"Surely to the worthy clerk, Bipin Dat," replied the beggar, innocently. "Many a time hath he cast a crumb to the afflicted."

Bipin scowled magnificently upon the beggar.

"Then seldom in future will the afflicted benefit by his compassion," he returned sternly, "unless they have more discernment than to style him a clerk. Know, thou fool, that he to whom thou criest is no longer a clerk, but hath so gained the ear of the noble Rani, that she hath appointed him to be her secretary."

His breast swelled with pride as he authoritatively announced his new rank.

"Secretary to the Rani," cried the beggar in astonishment. "Secretary to the Rani. Behold how God rewardeth the deserving. Protector of the Humble," he whined, "it was my infirmity that led me to make the mistake."

"Be careful then not to make such a mistake again," replied Bipin, mollified by the beggar's submissive tone.

He tossed a *pice* into the beggar's outstretched palm. Then, with lordly gait, he strutted on his way through the bazaars.

That Bipin Dat had become a man of authority was quickly impressed upon the friends and acquaintances he encountered. With condescending dignity he returned their effusive salutations, clearly intimating that a wide gulf of distinction lay between Bipin Dat the Rani's present secretary, and Bipin Dat the former ordinary clerk. Upon the children that sedately played in his path he frowned so threateningly that they shrunk back at his approach. He carried his head as if his turban already swept the clouds. In his mind the question uppermost was, to what height might his ascending star of fortune still further exalt the name of Bipin Dat.

At length he turned from the broad, booth-lined thoroughfare into a narrow alley, and directed his steps toward the door of a squalid house. He halted and knocked several times before he received an answer to his summons. The door was cautiously opened, and a woman appeared.

"Is thy learned husband, Mohurran Goshi, within"? he demanded.

"My honored husband is at present deeply engaged in compiling the horoscope of a noble raja," replied the woman, "but if you will enter, I will bear him a message."

"Aye, do thou tell him that the Honorable Bipin Dat, Secretary to the Rani, would engage his ear for a space. Thy husband hath already done me service."

At the woman's invitation he crossed the threshold of a bare and dingy room, the air of which was filled with a savory odor, rising from a pot placed upon a small fire. To this, Bipin directed his attention, that ever in close sympathy with his stomach, was alert to be interested in the progress of cooking.

The woman disappeared from view through an inner door.

After an absence of several minutes she returned with a reply. Her husband, though deep in study, would nevertheless receive so good a client as the Rani's secretary. Would he be pleased to pass into the other room?

Bipin followed the woman's direction and found himself in an apartment divided in the center by a curtain. There, seated upon the floor, the grave astrologer Mohurran Goshi, was surrounded by books and a variety of scientific instruments.

A STAR IN THE ASCENDENT

For some moments after Bipin's entrance the astrologer appeared too profoundly absorbed in his work to notice the presence of his visitor. At last he withdrew his gaze from an abtruse calculation, and directed a keen glance toward the face of the Rani's secretary.

"Welcome, worthy Secretary," he exclaimed. "Thou seest I prophesied truly. Yesterday a clerk, to-day a secretary; who knows, to-morrow thou mayest attain thy ambition and become a zemindar."

"A zemindar, forsooth!" cried Bipin, disdainfully. "Thou must know, learned Astrologer, that my ambition now rises beyond the station of a zemindar. A raja! Why not a raja"? he exclaimed, strutting back and forth. "Why should I not aspire to become a raja"?

"There is truly no reason, good Secretary," replied the astrologer, "why you should not become a raja, if the fates are propitious. Is not the great Maharaja Sindhia descended from a slipper-bearer"?

"To be sure," acquiesced Bipin, confidently. "I see no reason why I should not become a raja, and for that matter even a maharaja."

"Thou mayest even become a king," suggested the astrologer, with a note of sarcasm in his voice.

"Perhaps, who can tell, a king," agreed Bipin, reflectively. "But not too great a jump at first, learned sir. One might become a trifle dizzy. At present I will beg of thee to cast thy eye into the future and see if I am in the right way to become a raja. To that end, is the moment propitious for my taking upon myself the duties of the Rani's secretary"?

The astrologer glanced slyly toward his client.

"For such work," he explained, "the fee is necessarily higher than it was in forecasting your path toward the position of a zemindar. The deeper an astrologer is required to penetrate into futurity, the larger is the sum he is compelled to ask for his services."

"Speak not of that," returned Bipin, grandiloquently. "You may suppose that all the spoil of the Foreigners did not escape my fingers. Name thy fee for disclosing my way to become a raja."

The astrologer trading upon his client's vanity, named an extravagantly high figure. For a moment Bipin winced, but producing the money, he urged the astrologer to lose no time in the matter.

For a space, the astrologer pored over a chart of the heavens, muttering to himself unintelligibly; while Bipin impatiently awaited the result.

At last the astrologer spoke in an abstracted manner.

"Thy way to become a raja, O Secretary, is clearly revealed, but in thy path there stands a powerful enemy, who is even now within the palace of the Rani."

Bipin's countenance lengthened considerably.

"Is it that accursed pundit, Krishna Lal"? he asked.

"His name is not so written upon the heavens," returned the astrologer, "though its exact lettering I cannot as yet discern. But he is himself a raja and detesteth thee with all his soul."

"Blessed Devi"! exclaimed Bipin, with nervous apprehension. "What raja is there in the Rani's palace who beareth me so much ill-will. I know of no such one."

"So far he hath screened his animosity under a mask of kindness," replied the astrologer, returning to a scrutiny of his chart. "But thy path is clearly set in contradiction to his own. When they meet thou wilt be in danger of bodily harm. Thou wilt not lose thy life," he added, reassuringly, "but thou mayest be deprived of some of thy organs—thy nose, and possibly thy ears, good Secretary."

"Holy Kali," cried Bipin, impulsively raising his hand to his terror-stricken face. "At such a price I have no desire to be a raja. Nay, if such a danger encompasses me, the Rani may find another secretary."

"Patience, patience, good sir," continued the astrologer. "I did not say that there was no way of warding off these evils. By following such advice as I can give thee, thou mayest escape them all and yet live to be an unmaimed raja."

"Tell me how, I pray thee, O learned Astrologer," besought Bipin, with little trace of his importance remaining.

The astrologer appeared to reflect deeply before he replied:

"First, thou wouldst do well," he enjoined, "to remain in thy present service, because even if thou wert to fly to the end of the earth, that which is written on the heavens is bound to come to pass. But do thou carefully take note of everything in the palace, reporting each event to me from time to time, so that when thy evil moment approaches I can place before thee a sure defense. Especially do thou regard the actions of a Hindu noble recently arrived to join the Rani's cause. His looks I like not, though they be fair outwardly."

" Thou canst not mean the Raja Prasad Singh "? asked Bipin, in astonished accents.

" His name I cannot read as yet," returned the astrologer, " but if his image rises to thy mind from what I say, be assured he is the one who seeks to do thee so much injury."

Then the astrologer put a question pointedly.

" Of this Raja Prasad, of whom you speak. Does he stand close to the person of the Rani "?

" He is ever at her side," replied Bipin. " He seeks to be appointed to the command of the troops in Jhansi."

The astrologer shook his head gravely.

" Come to me again shortly," he concluded. " Then I will disclose to thee further. Remember to do as I have counseled thee."

As the astrologer appeared to be about to withdraw himself again into a state of profound abstraction. Bipin promised to return at an early date. With misgiving in place of elation in his heart, he left the house dejectedly.

" It seems to me," he reflected, as he made his way thoughtfully along the alley. " It seems to me I have gained little satisfaction by visiting that astrologer. For twenty rupees I have found out that the Raja, Prasad

Singh, is an enemy who seeks to possess himself of my nose and ears. Twenty rupees is a large sum to pay for such information. What evil things might not the astrologer have disclosed for fifty rupees? As to Prasad Singh, he is evidently jealous of my influence with the Rani. I must keep a close watch on him, and report to the astrologer frequently."

Bipin had scarcely left the astrologer's presence, when the curtain was thrust aside and Ahmad Khan stood in the aperture.

"Well, noble sir," said the astrologer, "I think I reduced that fool to a pliable state for our purpose."

Ahmad laughed sardonically.

"It is well," he replied. "No doubt his fears will temper him into a useful tool. To-morrow I return to the Rani's court in a new character. Keep my counsel, O Mohurran, and thou shalt receive better pay than thou ever didst before in thy musty calling, well recompensed as I note it is. One thing we have gleaned from his chatter. It was that dog of a Prasad who advised the Rani to play me such a trick. He aspires to become commander of the troops, does he? Well, he will yet be obliged to seek his appointment at the hands of Ahmad Khan, Raja of Jhansi."

Chapter V

AHMAD RETURNS TO COURT

THE rains had burst over India with terrific force. Even the arid and ever drought threatened State of Jhansi received a deluge. This soon rendered the main lines of communication impassable, and cut Jhansi off from the outside world.

Rumors only of stirring events reached the Rani's ears. In that mysterious way, by which news in India seems to filter through inanimate channels, she heard of the Foreigner's advance upon Delhi; but of the course which they intended to pursue toward her own State, she could obtain no reliable information. It appeared as if their desperate need to strike a blow at the center of the revolt would leave her unmolested for the present.

This was satisfactory as it gave her time to prepare for their return. But her position was still precarious from danger near at hand.

In the city of Jhansi her authority was now unquestioned, even though the rivalries among her retainers made it a delicate matter to enforce. But in the remaining parts of the State, the nobles, uninfluenced by her personality, were not so ready to submit to what they were inclined to regard as the capricious rule of a girl. From similar instances they feared the advent to power of some court favorite. More than one, also, had claims of his own to urge forward to the prize that had fallen into the Rani's grasp. With native caution they had waited for the result of the *coup d'état* before irrevocably declaring their own hands.

Thus, with the exception of a few minor nobles, the Rani's proclamation of her accession had been received by the Jhansi rajas throughout the State in ominous silence. A disquieting report persistently reasserted that the Maharaja Sadescheo, a cousin of the late Raja of Jhansi was collecting troops near his fortress of Shahpur, for the purpose of joining forces with the Peshwa. This did not deceive the Rani's alert intelligence. A descent upon the city of Jhansi was, in her reckoning, the Maharaja's more probable aim.

Under these circumstances she had prudently secured the gates and ramparts of Jhansi with her own soldiers, leaving the fort and cantonments without the city in the possession of Ahmad Khan, whose sullen attitude she viewed with anxiety. While the Mohammedan noble seemed to possess every evil trait to which mortal flesh is heir, she fully appreciated the control of his ferocious bravery, as an awe inspiring weapon to hold over the heads of those who yet disputed her title.

His plea of sickness, as an excuse for his absence from her court, if a ruse to screen other motives, was not confirmed by any sign of action. She was led to hope, that by the use of subtle influence, his allegiance might be retained without making too great a sacrifice to his ambition.

How to accomplish this was the question of the hour. The Rani was seated in one of her private apartments discussing the news of the morning with Prasad, when Bipin entered. He paused within the door, and glanced suspiciously at the Hindu noble.

"Well, learned Secretary," greeted Prasad affably, "Thy face seems to reflect the scowl of the elements. Doth the weight of thy exalted office press too heavily upon thy turban"?

"Thanks to the Rani's graciousness," returned Bipin, "my turban rests lightly enough; and its folds well protect my ears," he added significantly.

"He shall not imagine," thought Bipin, "that I am not forewarned of his accursed design."

Prasad laughed good naturedly as he regarded the unusual size of the secretary's head covering.

"It is almost large enough to protect thy nose as well, good Bipin," he suggested.

The solemn expression on the secretary's face deepened as he received what he believed to be sure confirmation of the evil lurking in Prasad's mind.

"As the saying is, noble sir," he rejoined with an assumption of sage gravity. "He who looks well to the roof of his house need trouble little about an approaching storm."

"Truly Bipin, thou art a philosopher," remarked the Rani with a smile.

"Aye, always by thy favor, noble Lady," he answered.

"I keep a good watch not only upon my nose and ears, but upon all my other possessions."

The secretary concluded this passage of words with a wary look directed toward Prasad. He then advanced and delivered a missive to the Rani.

"From the Maharaja Sadescheo of Shahpur," he said, bowing. "A messenger hath just delivered it at the palace."

The Rani took the letter eagerly.

"Ah," she exclaimed. "Now we shall know whether Sadescheo's newly acquired martial spirit leads him to join the Peshwa. If I mistake not, his avarice prompts him to cast longing eyes upon the revenues of Jhansi. It is a treasure chest rather than honor which men like Sadescheo crave."

She hastily opened the letter and gathered its contents.

"Go," she cried with a commanding air, to Bipin. "Go, but remain within call, as I may need thy services."

When Bipin had retired, she handed the letter to Prasad.

"Read that, my Lord," she exclaimed. "We need no longer remain in doubt as to Sadescheo's reason for collecting troops. He reminds me that as the late Raja's cousin he is entitled to some voice in the settlement of affairs, and that until I have been proclaimed in a *Darbar* of the Jhansi nobles, he cannot recognize my right to inherit the throne. The fool! the fool"! she continued passionately. "How many of them are there to be taught that the power of Lachmi Bai doth not rest upon the will of nobles, but in her own spirit, and in the love of her people."

Prasad, in turn, read the letter, and then tossed it contemptuously from him.

"Who is this Sadescheo that presumes to question your authority"? he demanded.

"Oh," she returned with a gesture of disdain. "Maharaja Sadescheo possesses a fortress at Shahpur. He hath some followers; but he would never have dared to address me in this fashion had Ahmad Khan remained at my side. I fear he must have received some hint of the Mohammedan's defection."

"Ah! Ahmad Khan! Ahmad Khan"! Prasad ejaculated impatiently. "His name is ever sounding in my ears."

He rose abruptly and passed to one of the windows where he gazed angrily out upon the lowering clouds, that swept across the sky, at intervals drenching the land with cyclonic violence.

Then as if a resolution was suddenly formed in his mind, he returned to the Rani's side and besought her in fervent accents.

"Fair Rani," he cried. "Why speakest thou so much of this Ahmad Khan? Surely thou canst no longer hold him in thy favor. One look upon his surly countenance and thou beholdest treachery marked by every line. Of this, recently thou hast had ample proof. But give me, ah, dear lady, I implore thee, give into my hands the command of thy troops, and thou shalt see how quickly I will subdue this presumptuous Maharaja."

The Rani smiled approvingly upon his eager countenance, but shook her head negatively.

"Prasad, well do I believe in thy devotion and courage, but thou art hasty in judgment. Consider how rash would be thy action. Thou wouldst carry my troops away to Shahpur, and leave me—to whom wouldst thou leave the defense of the city? To Ahmad's soldiers? Nay surely! No," she added thoughtfully. "In my mind all such work without the city must fall to Ahmad's lot. But how to control his savage nature, for the moment, I see not clearly."

Prasad again paced to a little distance. An expression of keen disappointment settled on his face.

"Nay Prasad," she enjoined in a gentle voice. "Be not out of humor with me. Thou dost not rightly see these things. Thou dost not understand what bitter jealousy would be stirred up among my own people, if I gave to thee that which many worthy officers covet most. Ahmad may be a greater villain than even thou wouldst have him, but forget not he goes to battle with greater zest than to a banquet. Bloodshed and rapine are his calling, and few there are who do not shudder at his name. Ah! If I could only send him forth to this impertinent Sadescheo."

"Is it possible thou, too, art afraid of him"? suggested Prasad.

A laugh of derision escaped the Rani's lips.

"Lachmi Bai afraid of Ahmad—of anyone? Nay, you know her not, O Prasad."

The Hindu noble's intense jealousy prompted him to an ungallant retort. He turned quickly toward her and muttered between his clenched teeth:

"Perchance thou art in love with the Mohammedan"?

She rose to her feet and stood confronting him; her form quivering with emotion; her cheeks aflame; her eyes flashing threateningly; her breast throbbing with the insult.

"Dare not thou ever speak to me again such thought," she retorted sternly. "Dost think that I, of noble birth and lofty caste, would descend to gratify the passion of an accursed Moslem, even if he could place upon my head an empire's crown. Dost think—Ah, Prasad," she continued in a softer tone. "Thou art surely out of thy mind to speak thus to me. Thou hast forgotten that although I am the Rani, I am still a woman. I did not think this of thee."

Her voice quavered as the passion roused by the insult to her dignity gave place to a realization of the wound made, by one, for whom she had come to form a tender regard.

Prasad glanced at the eyes from which the fire had been quenched by gathering tears. He was seized with contrition, and cast himself abjectly at her feet.

"Ah! Beast that I am," he cried in accents of self reproach. "How dare I throw a doubt upon thine honor.

Forgive me. Forgive my folly, thou dear one. Surely thou knowest it is my love for thee, which maketh me hate the very name of any other uttered by thy matchless lips. I vow it is my only desire to do thee service, aye, if it be the will of God, to give my life for thee."

She rested a hand gently upon his shoulder, and gazed down upon him with affection.

"This time thou art forgiven," she returned. "But distress me not so again, my Prasad. Thou shall yet do me not unrequited service, if thou canst be unresentful of the means I am compelled to use to make my will obeyed. If thou seest me take in hand a two edged sword, be assured it is the best weapon I can find to parry disloyalty in both Hindu and Mohammedan."

"So be it, fair lady," he replied. "Thou art my will, my life."

He rose to his feet and for the moment was tempted by an uncontrollable desire to enfold her in his arms. He took a hurried pace forward, but the act was prevented by the entrance of a woman servant.

"My Lady Rani," the latter announced. "Ahmad Khan hath come to the palace. He urgently craves an audience with your Highness."

The Rani's face expressed welcome surprise.

"So," she cried. "Ahmad returns to caress the hand that sways his destiny. Fierce beast that he is. I—I am his mistress, aye, his master.

"Come," she added, beckoning to Prasad. "Be watchful of thy temper, O good friend."

When the Rani entered the room in which Ahmad was waiting, he saluted her with profound reverence. Thrice he made a courtly *salaam* at a respectful distance. In his outward manner there was no sign of the arrogance which had marked his last abrupt entrance into her palace.

Whatever conclusion the Rani drew from the glance directed toward him, she extended a friendly greeting. "Thou art welcome, Ahmad," she exclaimed, intimating her pleasure that he should draw nearer. "Thou art ever welcome to the Palace of the Rani. I trust thou art recovered from thy sickness."

"Noble Lady," he replied, as if with an effort. "The physician had enjoined a longer period of confinement to my room; but the news from Shahpur made me hasten to thy side."

The Rani started.

"Hast thou heard from Sadescheo then"? she asked wistfully.

"Of him rather than from him, noble Lady," replied Ahmad. "Sadescheo gathers troops about his fortress, so it is thy humble servant's advice that thou dost, without loss of time, dispatch a strong body to learn his reason."

The Rani turned a searching look upon the Mohammedan.

He met her gaze unflinchingly.

"Noble Rani," he petitioned. "Thou hast good cause to doubt my faith and word. But, gracious Lady, hear my explanation. True is it that Bahadur Shah com-

"Then will I set forth to bring this dog of a Maharaja to his senses?"—Page 57.

manded me to protect the Government of Jhansi, but surely for thy sake. My people were carried away by their zeal and triumph over the Foreigners. They were guilty of an offense against thy authority. In the same enthusiasm of the hour I, too, lost control of my proper reverence for thy person. For this, noble Rani, I do seek thy pardon; and as evidence of my regret, I beg that thou wilt direct me to march instantly with three hundred Afghan troopers, who have arrived this morning without the city, and demand submission of this Sadescheo. Be assured if he does not comply speedily, I will rout his people like sheep before a band of wolves. In chains, at my horse's hoofs, will I drag him and his relatives hither."

While Prasad gazed with wonder at the Mohammedan's altered manner, the Rani assured him that the past had already been forgotten.

"Then will I set forth for Shahpur, noble Rani," he asked, "to bring this dog of a Maharaja to his senses"?

"Not so hastily, my Lord," the Rani answered thoughtfully. "The sword once out of its sheath, the fight is on, and who knows what a turmoil we may stir up in the state. Wiser it would seem to me, to overawe Sadescheo by a display of greater force. How many people, think you, hath he already collected to his support."?

"Noble Lady," replied the Mohammedan, "I know, nor care not. But give to me the order and with a hundred Afghans to every thousand of his people few will remain in Shahpur to tell of Ahmad's visit."

"Ahmad, good friend," replied the Rani authoritatively. "That must not be. Well do I know and appreciate thy courage, but bloodshed among ourselves is what I strive to avoid."

"Better to crush the cobra before it raises its head," he remarked significantly.

"Aye, but I would rather that with thy Afghan horsemen, thou dost take an equal number of my troopers. Then will Sadescheo perceive that both Hindu and Mohammedan are united in my cause, and will submit without resort to force."

Ahmad appeared to coincide with her argument.

"Thou speakest ever wisely, O Rani," he returned. "But in such event might not I ask that the noble Prasad Singh here, doth lead thy troops, if he will deign the comradeship of so rough a man at arms."

Prasad looked up eagerly at the unexpected request, and implied compliment. He began to view Ahmad in a different light.

"With the Rani's permission, gladly will I do so," he acquiesced.

The Rani perceived that Prasad's presence with the expedition might act as a restraining influence, as well as a safeguard upon the Mohammedan.

She gave her consent readily.

"Thou wilt take three hundred of my horsemen," she addressed Prasad, "and accompany Ahmad Khan to Shahpur. Upon thy return a *Darbar* shall be held in which I will make the chief appointments in the state.

She then turned to Ahmad and asked if it would be possible for him to reach Shahpur in the present state of the weather.

"Fair Lady," replied the Mohammedan. "Have I not fought among the Afghan passes when the winter snows were tinged a bloody red. Have I not chased Kurd horsemen into their bleak fastnesses. Such squalls as these but refresh the mettle of our steeds. Fear not, at daybreak, Ahmad Khan will break his fast with Sadescheo."

"Then farewell, my Lords," the Rani cried. "Go, terrify Sadescheo as much as thou wilt, but, remember, draw not the sword unless thou art compelled as thou regardest my favor."

Ahmad saluted and retired first from her presence. Prasad was about to follow, when he paused a moment.

"What are thy commands"? he asked in a low tone, as if he expected an order yet to be disclosed.

"Be watchful," she replied. "For the present he may be trusted, because"—

A smile of triumph broke upon her face as she concluded—

"If thou dost love the Rani, remember her command."

She passed to a window and watched the two nobles mount their chargers. Her spirit was stirred by the sight of their martial bearing.

"Ah"! she sighed regretfully. "Ah! How I would like to be one of them. To be a man and ride forth sword in hand, to battle; to hear the cannon roar, and mingle with the clash of arms. Perhaps, who can tell, some day the Rani may command her troops in person."

Then her thoughts took another channel.

"Sadescheo," she exclaimed. "Sadescheo! Poor, foolish, coward. I have no fear how he will act when the dawn finds Ahmad demanding admittance, in my name, at the gates of Shahpur.

Chapter VI

THE OATH

FAITHFULLY Ahmad kept his word to the Rani. Through the black, tempestuous night, he swept over the road to Shahpur. He recklessly plunged into swollen torrents. He callously hurled himself upon whatever obstacles lay in his path. Whirlwinds and stormbursts seemed in sympathy with his furious nature, bearing him onward rather than impeding his progress. Struggling, swearing, crashing in his wake, the troopers followed as best they could. A horse falling through sheer exhaustion, rider and beast were left to extricate themselves. Another, carried away in the flood of a river, was, without a saving effort, abandoned to his fate. To Ahmad, such incidents were only manifestations of the Will of Allah, by which all men must die when their appointed hour had come.

This exhibition of splendid recklessness was not without effect upon the brave spirit of Prasad. With rigid features he strenuously spurred forward at Ahmad's side. In his mind there gradually formed an understanding of the value which the Rani placed upon the services of the Mohammedan. It was like a bolt of lightning held in reserve, a force to be controlled only with the greatest skill and prudence; yet one that launched forth, burning to destroy, and oblivious of meeting with destruction itself; a terrible and awe-inspiring object.

Seldom were words exchanged. A guttural oath occasionally burst from the Mohammedan's lips as he found his way momentarily blockaded; an exclamation of anger went forth upon the night as he glanced back over his shoulder to discover that his pace had outstripped that of his followers.

The sullen break of day found Ahmad Khan and his companions, shaggy, dirt begrimed, with sodden garments, emerging from a ravine. At the entrance, perched upon the summit of a rock, rose indistinctly in the misty half light, the gray walls of the citadel of Shahpur.

He halted his men for a short space to enable stragglers to rejoin the party, and to perform a religious act. In Ahmad's nature, there was mingled with an absolute lack of human principle, a strange leavening of superstitious reverence. The more villainous the project upon which he was bent, the more scrupulous would he be in conforming to certain outward observances of his religion. If a murder was to be accomplished by the basest treachery, he would as fervently call down the blessing of Allah upon the act, as if another were about to sacrifice himself in some deed of true heroism.

He unrolled a small piece of carpet, and spread it upon the ground. Then he knelt with his face toward the west, and remained a few minutes in prayer.

"There is but one God and Mohammed is the Prophet of God," he solemnly ejaculated at its conclusion.

Several of his troopers added an amen.

He rose and remounted.

He then carefully inspected the company, arranging them in double file. This done to his satisfaction he cautiously led the way toward the mouth of the ravine, taking advantage of such cover as was afforded by the low underbrush and projecting spurs of rock.

Ahmad thus advanced into a narrow sinuous path leading up to the main gate of the citadel, when he pressed forward so rapidly and noiselessly, that he was demanding admittance of the keeper, before the watchers on the walls had discerned his approach.

"Open there," he shouted, "to Ahmad Khan and the noble Prasad Singh, bearing a message from the Rani of Jhansi."

Ahmad Khan! Ahmad Khan! A panic seized those within the gates roused from their slumbers by the stentorian voice of the Mohammedan.

"Open dogs," he thundered, as his summons failed of an immediate response.

"Noble lords," at last came a quavering rejoinder. "Maharaja Sadescheo yet sleepeth. The gates cannot be opened without his order."

"Wake him then," cried the Mohammedan. "By God's holy Prophet, time passes upon an urgent matter."

"Noble lords, that is impossible."

"Accursed jackals. Am I to batter down the gate. Go to thy master, and if thou wilt, lay all the blame on Ahmad Khan. He will awaken quickly, enough, if I mistake not," he added.

A short period elapsed, passed restlessly by Ahmad, when the voice was again raised within the gate.

"Maharaja Sadescheo extends greeting. He would welcome the noble Ahmad Khan and his followers but that the citadel is already over filled. If the noble Ahmad Khan will enter unattended, then will Sadescheo gladly see him."

Ahmad cast himself impulsively from the saddle.

"Thou wilt not accept this challenge, surely"? asked Prasad.

"Surely will I," the other retorted. "Thou wilt keep these fellows here, and if I do not return or send for thee within an hour, thou canst ask the reason by an assault upon the gate. But there is no danger."

He passed through the massive door and found himself in a courtyard filled with Sadescheo's recently collected soldiers. As he strode inward fearlessly, they fell back before his grim and martial bearing. His way made clear through these, he was conducted to a room in the interior of the fortress to await the Maharaja.

With soldierly instinct Ahmad stepped to a window that commanded a partial view of the defenses.

"A good position," he reflected, as his glance swept along the walls, "and worth holding if garrisoned by a handful of Mohammedans instead of this Hindu rabble. Sadescheo"!—

A smile broke upon his face.

"Sadescheo thinks to trick the Rani of Jhansi. By God! he little knows with whom he has to deal. She would make a fit wife even for the illustrious Dost Mohammed, the Lion of Afghanistan. I warrant there is more in that bewitching form than most give credit for. Thus, for the undoing of this accursed Prasad, will Ahmad for a time become her humble slipper bearer. Allah! what is it in the girl that moves a man in spite of himself."

A voice pronouncing his name interrupted the trend of his thoughts. He turned abruptly to confront a man of past middle age, whose weak features bore evidence of a life of sensual debauchery. With outstretched hands Sadescheo greeted the Mohammedan.

"Thou hast come unexpectedly, and apparently without waste of time upon the road, O Ahmad," he exclaimed, eyeing the Mohammedan's travel-stained attire. Then in a lower tone, "Hast determined to assist in ousting that chit of a girl from the Raj of Jhansi"?

Ahmad drew himself up to his full height as he replied haughtily.

"I have come from Her Highness the Rani to know the reason of your collecting troops, and to demand a recognition of her authority."

"Come! come! Good Ahmad," the other rejoined. "It is early in the day for pleasantry. It is a new thing for Ahmad Khan to joke."

"A joke," repeated Ahmad sternly. "By the Prophet's beard it is no joke. On the Koran I have sworn to support the Rani."

The feeble smile on Sadescheo's face gave place to an expression of dismay.

" Thou canst not mean this," he returned, " for but the other day thou didst send a messenger agreeing to our plans."

" And to-day," retorted Ahmad threateningly, " I come in person to denounce that same messenger as a liar. Briefly, good friend, it doth not suit Ahmad Khan to oppose the Rani for the purpose of uplifting Sadescheo."

" Then thou hast surely chosen an ill-fitting place to make the declaration," replied the Maharaja significantly. " Perchance Ahmad Khan may remain in Shahpur until he again finds it expedient to change his mind. He does not seem to be aware that he speaks within the walls of Sadescheo's fortress."

With a rapid movement Ahmad was at Sadescheo's side. Roughly he laid a firm grasp upon the Maharaja's shoulder, while his disengaged hand fell to the hilt of a dagger protruding from his girdle.

" Aye, and thou art in Ahmad's power," he muttered fiercely. " If he sees fit to change his mind, that is his affair. If he orders thee to throw open thy gates to his people, three hundred Afghans and as many of the Rani's troopers, impatient to enter, yea or nay, and summon hither his lieutenant, thou hadst better do it quickly, or he will open thy body and toss forth thy chicken heart to swine. Art willing to follow such advice, valiant Sadescheo "?

Sadescheo glanced timorously toward the open door. Within call were a dozen armed retainers who at the raising of his voice would rush to his assistance. But he knew full well that before they could reach his side, Ahmad's dagger would be buried a foot deep in his breast. If in turn, the Mohammedan were slain after he had made a pile of corpses to fall upon, that would be little satisfaction to him personally. He therefore called an attendant and gave the required order. For a moment the servant hesitated. "Go," cried Sadescheo nervously. "Go do my bidding, swiftly. What would you have now"? he asked of Ahmad.

"That my troops receive food and lodging for the day," replied the other, "and that on my return to Jhansi to-night my lieutenant, Suliman Abhas and a hundred Afghans replace your people on the walls of the citadel. Further, thou wilt proclaim the Rani in *Darbar* and hoist her banner on the gate."

To this Sadescheo made a gesture indicative of enforced compliance.

Presently, heavy footsteps in the passage announced the approach of Prasad and Ahmad's lieutenant.

Upon entering they glanced from Sadescheo, still held in Ahmad's grasp, to their leader, and waited.

With grim ceremony he presented them to the Maharaja.

Sadescheo bade them a reluctant welcome.

"With your permission, noble sir," suggested Ahmad,

"we will proceed to your hall of audience. There the Rani's title will be proclaimed, and we will rest upon our return to Jhansi."

Before an hour had passed the Rani of Jhansi's banner was flying beside that of Sadescheo, and Ahmad's troops had replaced those of the Maharaja on the walls.

That night the two nobles set forth on their return to the capital.

The burst of the monsoon in Jhansi had for the time passed over, so they rode leisurely through the clear atmosphere. First, they discussed the general prospects of the rebellion, then their successful descent upon Sadescheo, and lastly the condition of their personal affairs.

"You carried your life upon the blade of your sword, when you entered Sadescheo's fortress," remarked Prasad admiringly. "It was an intrepid act."

Ahmad laughed carelessly.

"In truth no," he returned. "There are some men, I grant you, with whom it would have been a venturesome thing to do. It would be a dangerous trick to play upon such a one as Dost Mohammed, whose valour and resource rise with the greater odds against him. But with this Sadescheo"—

He uttered an exclamation of contempt as he concluded:

"Upon him you have but to frown, and he shivers from his turban to his slippers."

They rode on in silence for some distance across a

wide plain, the troopers following in a long procession, phantom like by the light of the moon.

Ahmad, apparently deep in thought, at last spoke in a reflective manner.

"Thou art a fortunate man, friend Prasad. Providence hath undoubtedly taken thy affairs into her special keeping."

"How so"? the other asked. "If by casting obstacles at every turn of my way she is doing me good service, then only am I the most fortunate of men."

"Why, good comrade," returned Ahmad. "Is it not great fortune to stand so high in the beautiful Rani's favor. What could man desire more"?

Prasad turned a glance quickly upon the Mohammedan, but his companion's head was bent downward toward the pommel of his saddle.

"If I stand high in her favor," he replied, "then she well keepeth it a secret."

"Dost thou not count it a favor"? asked the Mohammedan, "to be appointed to the supreme command of her troops when many crave so honorable a post."

"She hath not appointed me to any office," replied Prasad, "except upon this expedition, which was owing to thy suggestion."

Ahmad raised his face upon which rested a well feigned look of surprise.

"Truly you astonish me," he exclaimed. "But the Rani is a prudent woman, and doubtless waits a favorable moment to give it to thee. At the *Darbar* she will probably pronounce thy name in honor."

"I doubt it much," returned Prasad, "though I grant you she is a mistress in the art of not making clear her mind."

"Tut, tut," ejaculated Ahmad soothingly. "Woman like, she is but playing with thee awhile. But I know well she holdeth thee in high esteem. How could she do otherwise than appreciate the gallantry of so fine a soldier. For me," he added indifferently, "I possess little influence with the Rani, and at any moment I may be called away to set the Emperor's house in order. But when I make my report of this little business, be assured I will not fail to keep thy name in mind. If a humble word of mine can do thee service, it shall not remain unspoken."

The eyes of the two men met in a steady gaze. Upon the Mohammedan's face stern and cold as it appeared, Prasad could detect no sign of hidden motive. He had yielded homage to the man's reckless valor; might there not, he argued, after all dwell beneath the rough exterior, a generous nature, carried away at times by mad impulse.

"If thou wouldst do this for me," he returned, "thou wilt have placed me under obligation of a life. To command the Rani's troops is now my great ambition."

For an instant a sarcastic smile flickered about the Mohammedan's lips. But it was gone before it could be detected.

"Gladly will I take an oath upon the holy book to do it," he answered. "These officers of the Rani are well enough, but they lack that proper martial spirit which, as a soldier, I have noted plainly in thy conduct. For myself, my aims now lie elsewhere than in Jhansi; but even were that not so, I would willingly yield to thee the office, as it is but right a Hindu noble should command the forces of a Hindu queen."

"Ahmad," Prasad cried enthusiastically. "I have done thee an injustice. More, I have ever done the same as those of thy religion. It is said a Moslem can never be a friend. Henceforth I vow that such is false."

Ahmad bowed his head in acknowledgment of the other's confidence.

"Everyone hath an enemy," he replied, "who will misrepresent a good intention. If influence of mine can do thee service, by the holy *Kaaba* I swear the Rani will go into *Darbar* with but thy name upon her lips.

"Come! The day breaks," he concluded, "and we are still some leagues from Jhansi."

Again he halted to dismount and pray with his face toward holy Mecca.

Ahmad's devotions were of short duration. He concluded with a petition to Allah to witness the truth in his heart. Then vaulting into the saddle, he drove his spurs into his horse's flanks. With arms glinting in the sunshine, at a canter, he bravely led the cavalcade.

Chapter VII

HOW AHMAD KEPT HIS OATH

AHMAD returned alone to the Rani's palace. To avert all suspicion of his conduct, he dismissed his Afghans to the cantonments on approaching the city. With the plea of furthering Prasad's interest, he had advised the Hindu noble to absent himself when the report of their expedition was made. It would be difficult, he explained, to properly advocate the claim of another, if the person chiefly concerned were present.

Prasad clearly perceived the force of the Mohammedan's suggestion. He relied implicitly upon the other's good faith, and readily acquiesced.

"Make my best *salaams* to the divine Rani," he enjoined Ahmad on parting, "and say that I will come to her side as soon as I have changed my attire for garments more suitable to the presence of a queen."

Ahmad vowed that he would leave no compliment unsaid on Prasad's behalf.

"In truth," he reflected, as he proceeded on his way, "I may be wrong, but this Rani of ours seems rather to prefer the smell of powder to the most delicate perfume of Teheran. I fancy the courtier finds less favor in her eyes than the man-at-arms. Ah what a treasure! What an *houri*. She must, by the God of Islam, she shall be mine, if I am compelled to play a hundred different parts in turn."

As Ahmad dismounted, the beggar who had petitioned everyone entering the palace that morning, ceased his cry for alms. He crouched further into his corner as instinct told him it was the fierce Mohammedan at hand—one whose boast was that he neither feared nor pitied any human being.

Ahmad remarked the beggar's action.

"Thou poor wretch," said he in a voice into which he threw as much compassion as he could assume. "Art dumb now as well as blind."

Surprise was depicted on the face of the beggar, who had learned by past experience to expect a curse if he ventured to address Ahmad Khan.

"Noble Lord," he faltered. "Is it truly the voice of the great Ahmad that I hear"?

"Whose voice else"? demanded the Mohammedan in return.

The beggar shrugged his shoulders.

"Lord I know not," he answered.

Ahmad cast a small coin at the beggar's feet, and ascended the palace steps.

On the porch Bipin had been an interested spectator of the scene.

"Blessed Devi," he reflected. "What next will happen. Perchance we shall behold Ahmad Khan robed as a *Mollah* calling his people to prayer, from the balcony of a minaret. Everyone seems to be what he is not. To think that the well-looking Prasad should possess so villainous a heart, and the black Mohammedan display compassion for the unfortunate."

Bipin was still in a most unhappy frame of mind. That morning another circumstance had occurred fraught with ill-omen. A white cat bereft of one eye had persistently endeavored to sharpen its talons in his legs. To fathom the significance of the beast's actions, Bipin had promptly repaired to his friend the astrologer, who for a monetary consideration, had assured his client that they betokened the swift unfolding of Prasad's design. As a consequence, Bipin had armed himself with an ancient and rusty flint lock pistol, the massive butt of which protruded from his waistband.

The weapon at once attracted Ahmad's notice.

"What," he cried with gruff humor. "What do I behold? The worthy Bipin Dat, the man of peace, armed for mortal combat."

"Illustrious Lord," returned Bipin gravely. "When every man goeth armed, he is a fool who doth not follow the prevailing fashion."

"True, O Secretary," returned Ahmad, laying a familiar though heavy hand upon the other's shoulder. "Come, I like thee all the better for thy display of spirit. Soon thou wilt be wielding a sword with the best Afghan in my troop."

"And why should I not," rejoined Bipin. "One need not be born in a fortress to make a good fighter."

Ahmad threw back his head and laughed heartily. "Bipin," he replied, "I am inclined to think thou hast mistaken thy calling. Thou shouldst have been a soldier. Come! I will beg a commission for thee from Her Highness, so that thou mayest win the title, *Singh.*"

"Not so fast, good sir," replied Bipin. "In dangerous times arms are well enough for protection, but he who makes a profession of exchanging blows receives too many for my liking."

Ahmad laughed again. "Well! well! Bipin," he exclaimed. "I make no doubt when the moment comes thou wilt acquit thyself with the best of us. But in the meantime I would see the Heaven endowed Rani."

Bipin turned, and beckoned Ahmad to follow. He led the way into the palace.

The Rani had feared that in spite of the solemn injunction she had laid upon Ahmad, his uncontrolled nature might have led him into some overt act against Sadescheo. She was relieved, early in the report, to learn, that he had managed to enforce her authority upon the Maharaja without igniting a racial conflagration within her territory.

"Ahmad," she cried with a display of satisfaction. "Thou hast done well indeed. How can I reward thy services sufficiently"?

"Noble Rani," he answered. "Thy approval of my actions is all the recompense I ask."

A momentary expression of added relief crossed the Rani's face.

She was afraid he might demand that which his soldierly

qualities entitled him to claim, but which she still hesitated to give.

"If all others were only like thee," she returned, "how much easier would be my lot, how much more secure would be our position."

"Fair Lady," resumed Ahmad. "My position is uncertain, for I know not how soon I may be called away to sharpen the blunted teeth of Bahadur Shah's overfed soldiers. Wrangling among themselves over the plunder that has fallen into their hands at Delhi, they will scatter to the jungle like a band of jackals at the voice of the Foreign hunter. But if Ahmad Khan might presume to offer the great Rani some advice in certain matters, he would consider himself well repaid for any service he has rendered."

"Gladly will I hear thee, friend Ahmad," acquiesced the Rani.

"Principally is it," continued Ahmad, "in reference to the offices thou wilt doubtless make in *Darbar* to-morrow. Above all things it would be advisable to appoint a commander of the troops, to whom both thy Hindu and Mohammedan subjects will look with respect and confidence. If thou hast determined this already, then will the voice of thy humble servant remain silent."

"No Ahmad," returned the Rani thoughtfully. "I have not done so as yet. That matter troubles me more than all else. There are so many worthy aspirants that it is difficult to select the one who would suit the office best. Willingly will I listen to thy advice."

"Then, noble Rani," Ahmad proceeded, "Taking into account the conflicting aspects of the question, the man to be chosen must possess more than one qualification. Courage and daring must first of all be his birthright, but equally important is a knowledge of military strategy —none the less valuable if intuitive rather than acquired by experience, and in which rapidity of action must be the outward manifestation of an alert mind. To these must be added firmness of character to enforce discipline even to the point of seeming cruelty, holding human life in his own person and in that of others as of no account when necessary, yet not unmindful of the needs of his soldiers whose affection he will thereby gain in return. If, further, he should possess youth and a gallant bearing it will be to his advantage, for the trooper is ever the more eager to follow a captain of distinguished presence. If he possesses these qualities, noble Rani, even though thy selection were to fall upon a comparative stranger to the state, be assured thou wouldst act most wisely. Such a one I dare to have in mind."

Unconsciously Ahmad had faithfully portrayed the character as yet undisplayed of the girl before whom he stood.

In the pause which ensued it was evident the Rani was mentally reviewing the faces of those known to her who would be most likely to coincide with Ahmad's description.

"Ah"! she exclaimed at last. "Dost thou refer to Prasad Singh"?

A look of slight astonishment broke upon Ahmad's face.

"Prasad Singh"! he ejaculated. "Noble Lady," he protested, "for aught I know to the contrary Prasad Singh *may* possess all these qualities and more. Untried in any important affair, he *may* prove to be a great captain, though in our little ride to Shahpur, but for the banter of his rough companion, I think he would more than once have turned back. But Prasad surely is a good comrade and a handsome fellow, even if his name doth not hover on my lips."

"Whose name dost thou have in mind, then"? asked the Rani somewhat perplexed.

"It is the young officer Dost Ali, noble Lady," replied Ahmad confidentially. "Thou wilt have heard his father was a Maratha who was driven into exile by the Foreigners, and dying left his young son to the protection of the illustrious Dost Mohammed. Brought up by such a leader, he has well learned the trade of arms. By birth a Hindu and a Mohammedan by adoption, both factions in the state might well unite to serve under him. Moreover, such action on thy part would surely please the great Amir of Afghanistan, some of whose troopers are now a part of thy forces, and whose doubtful attitude toward the Foreigners might thereby be determined in support of India's cause."

The Rani turned from Ahmad and gazed out of a window pensively. There was forming quickly in her mind an ulterior object that might be promoted by following Ahmad's suggestion. Among her older officers there was a marked disposition to regard her opinion in military affairs lightly, as that of a mere girl whose judgment in such matters could be of no value. A younger man, susceptible to her personal charm, would, she thought, be more likely to follow, unhesitatingly, the dictates of her will.

"Thou hast observed the young officer of whom I speak, my Rani"? Ahmad asked with a shade of anxiety in his voice, as he waited on her answer.

"Truly I have," she answered. "I have remarked him well several times. I like his manner and appearance. There is much discernment in what thou sayest. For a space I will think over it, and to-morrow make known my decision."

Ahmad *salaamed* low and withdrew from her presence.

So far, he was satisfied with the favorable view the Rani seemed to take of his covert plan of installing a *protégé* of his own in one of the most important offices of the government, and the deeper project of eventually destroying his rival by that means.

The Rani proceeded to an inner court, and called her chief waiting woman to her side.

"Rati," she began. "I am curious to know what other women—the ladies of the *zananas*—think of me. Tell me, O Rati, thou who learnest such things, what is the opinion in such places of Lachmi Bai"?

The girl looked nonplussed.

" Speak truly," enjoined the Rani. " Flattery enough I can have for the wish."

The girl's uneasiness increased visibly.

" Noble Rani. They say. They say "—she hesitated.

" Yes, what do they say "? the Rani demanded impatiently.

" That thou art well gifted, O noble one," the girl replied evasively.

The Rani turned a look of displeasure upon the girl. " I did not ask for that," she spoke authoritatively. " Tell me what else do they say of me "?

" Some affirm that thou art as beautiful as the opening lotus, but others "—

The girl broke off timidly.

" Others," concluded the Rani with a smile. " Others are afraid for their sweethearts, aye Rati "?

" Perchance, noble Lady," acquiesced the girl.

The Rani's humor displayed itself in a silvery laugh that was echoed by the walls of the court.

" Rati," she commanded, " what more do they say "?

" O great one," petitioned the girl, " urge me not in this manner, lest thou become offended."

" Offended surely will I become unless thou doest as I bid thee."

The girl paused a moment, then proceeded fearfully.

" They say, O Rani, that thou art vain of thy beauty, and forgettest thy modesty as a Hindu woman by so openly consorting with soldiers and gallants."

"Say they so," the Rani cried passionately, stung to the quick by the implication.

The girl fell at the Rani's feet and implored her not to visit punishment upon an unwilling offender's head.

"Pardon, O Queen. Thou didst force me," she besought fervently.

"I am not angry with thee, poor girl," the Rani replied in a softened tone. "But while my actions are seen by all, to what do many of these *zanana* beauties stoop? The shutters of their windows can best tell. I will show them, these women of such fine sensibilities, how the Rani, for all her pride, observes a custom too much falling into disuse among the rich and great. I have heard that my honored *guru* [1] cometh to aid me with advice, that he even now approaches Jhansi. Go, therefore, order my bearers, so that I may go forth to receive him with all the respect due his office.

The girl rose, and departed to obey the Rani's behest.

The Rani raised a hand wearily to her forehead.

"So much discussion to appease," she murmured, "so much jealousy and envy among those who should assist, rather than thwart the only one who dared to do what has been accomplished. Love! Ah, only it seems do the poor and afflicted truly love the Rani. Even Prasad, who vows by all things sacred that my image beatifies his sleep, hath ever a favor uppermost in mind."

Presently a state *duli*,[2] with curtains to screen the oc-

[1] Spiritual teacher. In its nearest interpretation, Godparent.

[2] A kind of sedan chair.

cupant from view, was carried to the entrance of the palace.

To the surprise of her servants the Rani came forth without her *burkha,* or long mantle, invariably worn by native ladies of rank to conceal the whole person in public.

She promptly ordered the curtains of the *duli* to be removed.

For a moment her servants hesitated to comply. Never before did they recollect such an order to have been given.

"What," she cried. "Dost thou not hear my command? Take those hangings away. I am not a Mohammedan, but a Hindu Rani in my own right. Of old time our princesses were not afraid to show their faces to the people. It is my pleasure that they shall know well the features of Lachmi Bai."

The curtains were hurriedly removed. The Rani entered her chair, and surrounded by her servants was borne in the direction of the city gate, through which it was expected her *guru* would enter.

At the head of the procession, the worthy secretary, Bipin Dat, marched with pompous dignity. Against all contingencies, he had prudently further armed himself with a long sword, that trailed in the dust at his side, and made him an awe inspiring object to the beggars that chanced in his way.

As the procession passed through the streets, the people saluted the Rani with terms of affection. Many turned to catch a glimpse of her face.

"See," they cried. "The Rani of Jhansi fears not the gaze of our eyes."

It had gone little more than half the distance to the gate, when it was met by a bullock cart in which rode an old man of venerable aspect.

The Rani seemed to instantly recognize his features. She commanded her bearers to halt.

"It is my dear *Guru,*" she cried. "Ah, how glad I am to see him."

On his part the old man recognized the rich liveries of the servants as those of his godchild, the Rani. With an effort he dismounted from his cart and would have prostrated himself before her, had she not anticipated his action.

She alighted quickly and knelt at his feet. She embraced them affectionately, and cried in a voice which all might hear:

"O *Guru,* live forever. Grant a blessing to thy godchild, Lachmi Bai."

For a moment the old man's face reflected the astonishment of the crowd that had gathered. That she should thus humble herself in public was certainly a surprising act. But its significance was not lost upon the people, who, as the old man raised her in his arms tenderly, called down a thousand blessings on her head.

The first greetings over, the *Guru* was about to again climb into his rickety vehicle, when the Rani interposed. She insisted that he take her place in the *duli.*

At first, the old man demurred at so great an honor being accorded him. But the Rani was persistent.

"Before, I have ever met thee, dear *Guru,*" she cried, "as but a poor captive in Jhansi. Now that I am the Rani, I desire my people shall see I am not unmindful of the ancient customs of our race."

Thus she followed on foot behind her *Guru's* chair, as the procession returned to the palace.

Chapter VIII

THE DARBAR

THE great hall of the palace presented a splendid, an imposing spectacle. Its pillars were decorated with banners and trophies, its walls hung with rich draperies from the looms of Kashmir and Sind. At the further end a throne of ivory inlaid with silver and mother-of-pearl, was placed under a gorgeous canopy. It stood upon a platform approached by a short flight of steps, covered with a Benares carpet of black velvet embroidered with gold thread. The subdued light, the atmosphere of antiquity, that pervaded the audience chamber of the Rani of Jhansi, enforced that reverential feeling, by which the human voice naturally sinks into a whisper.

As yet the throne was unoccupied.

In the body of the hall were groups of magnificently attired maharajas, rajas, and military officers, awaiting the entrance of the Rani. Diamonds blazed in turbans of many colors, ropes of pearls hung about their necks, rubies, emeralds, and sapphires, scintillated in barbaric profusion amid the gold embroidery of their robes of state.

Amid these dazzling personages, Ahmad Khan, the humble servant of God, was a conspicuous figure by the simplicity of his martial uniform. In his new character he had evidently curbed his passion for outward display. In place of jewels he had mounted a green badge in his turban, as a sign that he was one among the Faithful who had obeyed the commandment of the Prophet and made the pilgrimage to the Holy City. Slung from his shoulder was a plain leather band suspending a sword encased, also in a plain leather sheath. But the sword was as sharp as the arm was strong to wield it. He gazed proudly round upon the throng. Was there any man who cherished evil in his heart? If so, his enemy was careful to display no outward sign of animosity.

Indeed, it was the knowledge that this awe inspiring warrior had openly espoused the Rani's cause, the report of his descent upon Sadescheo, carried swiftly to the boundaries of the state, that had brought many wavering nobles in haste to tender their allegiance at the first *Darbar* of the Rani.

Among the last to enter the hall before the hour set for the council was Prasad Singh. He had undoubtedly spent much time and thought in arraying his handsome form to striking advantage. A diamond aigrette rose from the folds of his turban directly above his forehead. A collar of emeralds encircled his neck, his long outer garment was stiff with embroidery, the velvet scabbard of his sword was encrusted with gems.

Ahmad who seemed to have been watching for Prasad, at once strode to the Hindu noble's side and greeted him with every outward mark of friendship.

He drew Prasad apart and spoke in an undertone to avoid being overheard.

"This is thy day, O Prasad," he said congratulatingly. "Thou wilt be reckoned as among the most fortunate of men. Thou mayest prepare thyself to receive the felicitations of both those who wish thee well and those who envy thee."

Prasad returned the Mohammedan's salutation responsively.

"What did the Rani say," he asked, "when thou spoke to her of me"?

"What could she say," replied Ahmad, in a tone as if he had advocated the other's cause so well that there could be but one conclusion drawn. "What could she say! I swear never did eloquence so flow from my tongue in any man's behalf, as it did for thee, my Prasad. I vowed to the Fair One that the appointment thou seekest should by every right be thine. Upon the Holy Book I swore that but for thy dash and bravery, even the war scarred veteran, Ahmad Khan, might have been compelled to turn his back before the fury of that night of storm, and the strength of Sadescheo's frowning walls."

Prasad's gratitude manifested itself in a warm tribute to the other's friendship.

"But," he protested with a slight accent of concern, "I fear thou mayest have performed thy task too well, O Ahmad."

"Not I," returned the other. "Fear not that one who

has trod the pavement of the Afghan court has not learned to pick his way most warily. Be assured thy desire is already granted."

A sound of distant music broke upon their ears.

"Hark"! enjoined the Mohammedan in a whisper. "Hark! The Rani cometh to *Darbar*."

As the music drew nearer the nobles ranged themselves on either side of the hall leaving a passage in the center for the Rani and her attendants to approach the throne. A profound silence fell upon the brilliant assembly.

Nearer rolled the sound of an inspiriting martial air. Presently amid a loud clash of cymbals and the beat of drums, the foremost of the procession swept into the hall. Fans of peacock feathers waved aloft, emblems of state were borne before her to whom all eyes were directed.

"The Rani, the Rani," passed in an impressive whisper from mouth to mouth. In turn, each of the nobles made a low obeisance.

She walked with a stately, measured pace, a little apart from the rest of her suite. As she moved along the human aisle, the earnest expression on her beautiful features gathered an abstracted look, as if the thunder of the music crashing upward to the roof, carried her vision beyond the brilliant spectacle of the moment, to some perspective scene yet to be unfolded.

For the occasion she had robed herself with great magnificence after the Mohammedan rather than the Hindu fashion of ladies of high rank. Her reason was, perhaps, that it afforded her a better means of impressing those to whom a sumptuous display of jewels and fine raiment formed a considerable part of their existence.

In place of the simple, graceful *sari,* she wore an outer garment of scarlet cloth of gold, disclosing beneath, silken skirts of delicate hues and of such filmy texture that one might have supposed it was by a miracle the intricate embroidery of pearls had been stitched upon the material. Upon her head there rested lightly a cap of scarlet velvet set with pearls, that contrasted with the dark color of her gathered tresses. Pearls, lustrous, priceless pearls, adorned her neck, her ears, even her slippers. Upon her fingers, diamonds of Golconda served to draw attention to the symmetry of her hands.

"In the Paradise of the Prophet," murmured Ahmad as she passed, "could there be found such a one"?

Following in the Rani's train, the worthy secretary, Bipin Dat, marched with a lofty air, as if he trod upon the necks of the nobles present. His glance chanced to rest upon Prasad Singh. An inward tremor caused his spirit swiftly to descend to earth.

He hastily grasped a talisman that he had purchased from his friend the astrologer at great cost, and muttered a prayer.

"May holy Devi protect her servant from the accursed designs of the evil one."

The Rani approached the throne and seated herself with quiet dignity. On her right, the aged man, to whom she had accorded so great honor on the previous day, took up his station. Behind her, grouped themselves the personal retinue of her court.

The music ceased. Amid the silence which ensued, Ahmad Khan strode forward to the lowest step of the throne. He *salaamed* thrice before the Rani, then turned, and in a loud voice proclaimed her title.

"Behold," he cried. "The Pearl of Jhansi, the noblest of our Queens. Long live the fair Rani, Lachmi Bai."

The nobles gravely echoed the Mohammedan's salutation.

Then, one by one, they came forward, and were in customary form presented. They returned after the ceremony to chairs of state, or to seats upon the rugs spread on either side of the throne.

For each she found a suitable expression of greeting, but to Prasad she spoke in a gentler tone, and bade him take a place of honor at her hand.

"What did I tell thee," whispered Ahmad aside to him.

The Mohammedan had also been similarly favored by the Rani.

"What did I tell thee, friend. But I do not blame thy qualms. Lover like, thou canst not see a flower open until it is in full blossom."

A smile of gratification lit up Prasad's face, clouded for a moment as the Rani singled out the young Dost Ali, to stand upon the dais.

The presentations over, the Rani then rose to address the gathering. She spoke quietly but in her voice there was an unmistakable note of authority. It penetrated clearly to the furthest recesses of the hall.

First, she graciously thanked the nobles for their response to her summons to the *Darbar,* and their spontaneous recognition of her sovereignty. In return she assured them that her one aim was to promote the welfare of her state and people, that to everyone should be secured justice in his person and property.

"I who had suffered so much in that respect," she cried, "can never be unmindful of the misfortunes of others."

She then proceeded to confirm the nobles in all their ancient rights and privileges, and reviewed the situation as it related to the cause of India as against that of the Foreigners. The news from Delhi, she regretted to inform them, was unsatisfactory. Disrupted by internal dissension, the position of Bahadur Shah was fast becoming desperate, in the face of the investment of the city by the Foreigners. It was surely a warning to them in Jhansi, she declared emphatically, to submerge all personal animosities in the common object of defending to the death, the freedom they had regained with so much difficulty. She had, the Rani further related, dispatched trustworthy messengers to urge speedy action, on behalf of the cause, upon the powerful Maharajas, Gækwar of Baroda, Sindhia of Gwalior, and the great Mohammedan Nizam of Haidarabad. There was little reason to doubt that if they could only be persuaded to follow the unmistakable sympathy of their troops and people, Delhi might yet be preserved to the Emperor, and the Foreigners driven into the sea.

"But, my Lords," she cried, "we, at any rate, must prepare ourselves to defend the State of Jhansi against enemies from whatever direction they may come. The fortresses that have fallen into decay under the dominion of the Foreigners must be repaired speedily. New cannon must be cast forthwith and mounted on the walls. Ammunition and stores of grain above all our likely needs accumulated, and more troops raised to guard the passes. With your loyal co-operation, I have no doubt this necessary condition of affairs may be brought about with little waste of time."

The Rani paused for a short space; an interval that was utilized by her hearers in expressing their approval of her words.

At the commencement of her address they were impressed by her beauty and dignity; but as she proceeded amazement at her clear perception of the danger and needs of their position, gave place to all other feelings. More than one exclaimed:

"Truly the voice of Lachmi Bai is that of a great Rani."

With a motion of her hand she regained their attention, and continued:

"My Lords," she said. "To direct our best efforts for the end I have explained, there must above all things be established a firm central government in Jhansi. Not that I aspire to deprive any noble of his rule within his own district, but all authority must emanate from the throne it is mine by right to occupy. For this purpose certain officers of government must be appointed."

Ahmad's countenance remained impassive, while Prasad's gathered a look of eager expectancy.

"It is," the Rani continued, "partly to gain your approval of such appointments that I have called you to this *Darbar*. By such action, I trust, no jealousies will be aroused, no mistakes made that will stir up internal discord."

She paused for a moment, but as the countenances of the nobles thus far indicated approval of her words, she resumed.

"First, it is my desire that my honored *Guru* present, whose advice hath ever been of great benefit to me since my childhood, shall occupy the office of minister of state. In choosing him, you all know I am but following many ancient precedents, whereby *Gurus* of kings and princes have, by their wisdom, added luster to the crowns worn by their godchildren. Have I your approval of the appointment"?

Perhaps for the reason that no one particularly aspired to the office, perhaps because they might have thought there was little to be feared in the person of the venerable form at the Rani's side, the reply came unanimously, that the Rani's worthy *Guru* should be appointed her minister of state.

"It is well, my lords," she cried. Now to a more difficult matter. It must be known to you all that an army without a chief commander, whose orders must be obeyed by everyone without question, is a mere rabble in the face of the enemy. But the difficulty in Jhansi is, that all my officers are so brave and competent, that to single one out from amongst the others for the high honor in my gift, is an impossibility. I have, therefore, to suggest a remedy in this way."

She moved forward to the edge of the dais and stood before them, a majestic figure.

"My Lords," she cried, stretching forth an arm. "I, Lachmi Bai, the Rani, will command the forces of the State. If anyone doth say me, nay, he hath the right to let his voice be heard in council. I will listen to him patiently."

At critical moments in the lives of those destined to play heroic parts in the eyes of their fellow creatures, it not infrequently happens, that nature appears to cast a vote in their favor, by a striking manifestation of sympathetic accord. To many, such may be no more than coincidences, but to some, particularly to the Oriental, they are fraught with deep significance.

The sun mounting over the Palace discovered a rent in the awning of one of the windows set in the roof of the *Darbar* hall. It sent forth a shaft of dazzling light that, penetrating the darkened chamber, descended full upon the form of the Rani of Jhansi. In her robes of state, for the moment, she appeared in a blaze of splendor, that to her audience betokened a supernatural power guiding her destiny. Against such, what was man, that he should dare to raise a voice in protest? Was it not clearly a sign that the blessing and protection of the great God rested on her head. Even to Ahmad Khan, surprised and dumbfounded by the Rani's unexpected action, as seeming to again baffle his carefully laid plans, the incident was not lost upon his sense of superstition. Prasad's mind merely reflected the feelings of the others. A profound silence followed the Rani's declaration. No man ventured a yea or nay.

The Rani waited patiently a few moments for their answer, then again spoke.

" By your silence, my Lords, am I to gather your consent " ? she asked.

A Raja rose from his chair of state and replied:

" Surely thou art the Rani," he exclaimed. " Is it not the will of God that thy word shall be a law with us. Thou art the commander of us all."

" It is the will of God," came without a dissenting voice from all parts of the hall. " Aye, it is the will of Mahadiva."

The Rani warmly thanked the nobles for their confidence. She again eulogized their valor and loyalty, assuring them that when the moment of danger threatened, she would not be found wanting in courage, if necessary, to lead her army in person. So gentle yet so stirring was her appeal, that even the hearts of those before given over to sensual indulgences, were moved to do brave actions in her behalf.

They sprang to their feet and shouted enthusiastically.

"Thou art our Rani. We will follow thee to the death, O Queen of Jhansi."

An expression of surpassing happiness rested on her face.

"Then, my Lords," she cried, "I bid you all attend me to-morrow when I will repair in state to the White Turret, and raise upon it my banner as the emblem of my military authority."

"And let him who dares," she concluded, "lift his hand against it."

The walls trembled with the applause which her concluding sentence and her defiant air brought forth.

Again she enjoined silence by a gesture.

"Before the *Darbar* closes," she added, "I have yet to speak a word to you. With much thought I have decided that the well tried valor of the noble Ahmad Khan, entitles him to the subordinate command of the forces quartered in the cantonments, as long as he shall remain in Jhansi. Further, for certain reasons, I will appoint as my lieutenant of Jhansi, the noble, Dost Ali, lately come to us from the great Amir of Afghanistan, Dost Mohammed."

Briefly she recapitulated the reason urged by Ahmad Khan for the Dost's appointment to the greater office. No voice dissenting she then declared the *Darbar* closed.

Kindly she turned to Prasad and invited him to accompany her to her private apartments.

With intense chagrin, jealousy, and disappointment in

his heart, he bowed haughtily, and pleaded as an excuse a pressing matter requiring his presence elsewhere.

For a moment a look of pain crossed her face.

But the music again sounded, the fans of state waved on high, the procession re-formed, and between the ranks of *salaaming* nobles, the Rani retired from her first *Darbar*.

Ahmad Khan had scarce time to adjust his plans to the unexpected course taken by the Rani. But in the appointment of his *protégé*, even to the lesser position of honor, he beheld a dagger by which to stab his rival's favor with the Rani, a fatal blow.

Prasad strode toward the door, wrapt in gloomy, bitter feelings, without exchanging a parting salutation with anyone.

Ahmad followed quickly and caught up with the Hindu noble before the latter had crossed the threshold.

" Stay, good friend," he cried. " Thou art in a great hurry to shake the dust of the *Darbar* hall from thy feet."

" Aye," returned the other, with sullen ill humor. " And it will not be long before I shake the dust of the accursed city from my feet."

" Why so " ? asked Ahmad with assumed astonishment.

" Why so," retorted Prasad angrily. " How canst thou ask, why so, after thy cajolery " ?

Ahmad shrugged his shoulders deprecatingly. " Friend, Prasad," he asserted. " I give thee my word, no man in the *Darbar* was more astonished than Ahmad Khan when the Rani grasped the sword of state herself.

For once he spoke the truth honestly.

"Of that I make no complaint," retorted Prasad. "If the Rani so wished it, hers was the prerogative; though a strange one for a woman to assert."

"Then to what hast thou taken so much offense"? asked the Mohammedan with apparent innocence.

Prasad, in turn, regarded Ahmad with a look of astonishment.

"Art thou so guileless, O Ahmad Khan"? he asked, "after all that has passed between us, not to imagine that I might be offended with the Rani's action, in giving to another—a stranger—that which she knew I besought of her favor."

"Ah! as to that, my Prasad," returned Ahmad, pacifically, "there may have been many reasons in the Rani's mind, apart from the chief one given. She may have assumed thou wouldst not have cared for the lesser honor conferred upon Dost Ali—by the way a handsome fellow too; or, woman like, mind, I say no word against the beauty, wisdom, and courage of the Rani, she may have admired the gallant bearing of this fellow. A new favorite, perchance. Thou must remember, good Prasad, she is a woman as well as Rani, and turneth her gaze first upon one, then toward another."

Prasad's brow scowled threateningly.

"By God," he muttered. "She shall not treat me so."

"Nay, nay, Prasad," Ahmad rejoined restrainingly.

"Thou canst not dictate to the Rani. She would care little even if thou didst menace her with a sword. With her thou must fence with other weapons. I make no doubt it is but a passing fancy she hath conceived for this Dost Ali."

"Dost Ali"! Prasad muttered fiercely, "Dost Ali! Dost Ali had better look to the sharpening of *his* sword."

"Come! come, good Prasad," continued Ahmad, laying a friendly hand upon the other's arm. "Dost Ali hath no weight in the Lovely One's esteem. But display thy spirit and she will quickly turn again to thee, for she loveth thee in her heart, I could swear to it. Be advised in this way. Absent thyself from the ceremony of to-morrow. I will tell her I know not what ails thee, that thou art falling sick, perchance. Then behold how she will fly to thy side. Then see how speedily she will grant anything thou askest."

"Ahmad," the other returned gravely. "I know not what to think of thee. Thy ways here may win for thee the Seventh Heaven of thy Prophet's Paradise, or the lowest pit of his Inferno. But thou givest shrewd advice, I make no doubt."

Ahmad laughed. "Come, friend," he rejoined. "Clearly thou dost not understand a woman's ways. She delighteth in men striving for her favor, but let the chosen one display indifference, and she is at his feet. In the meantime let us to my house without the city. There," he added insinuatingly, "thou wilt discover a little treasure that may amuse thee—a Kashmir dancing girl of no ordinary charm, my Prasad. True her eyes, her lips, her form, are not comparable to the endowments of the superb Rani, but she hath a way with her that pleaseth many. Some of the *Giours'* spirits have I, too; and though as one of the Faithful I may not taste of such, yet thou mayest in their subtle waters, forget the passing cloud until the sun shall again blaze upon thy turban. Come! Let us away, and forget our disappointments. All will yet go well with thee."

To this proposal, after some demur, Prasad reluctantly consented.

With a courtly bow that concealed the sinister smile upon his face, Ahmad motioned the Hindu noble to take precedence of him, by passing first out of the *Darbar* hall.

Chapter IX

AT THE HOUSE OF AHMAD KHAN

THE house of Ahmad Khan, with numerous outbuildings, was situated in a large compound, pleasantly shaded by willows, and overlooking the placid waters of the lake that stretched over a wide expanse to the eastward of the city. Both externally and internally its atmosphere suggested the impression that the owner was not averse to a comfortable, even a luxurious retreat after the hardships and dangers of his military exploits.

If the stables filled with high-bred chargers, the walls decorated with a splendid collection of trophies, and the large retinue of armed servants unmistakably emphasized the profession of Ahmad Khan; the shaded halls, luxurious divans, and the soft rugs woven in rich colored arabesque patterns, told that he possessed other tastes than those pertaining to the field of battle.

To Prasad he remarked these evidences of another life apologetically.

"For Ahmad Khan, O Prasad," he said, "the step of a mosque, or the bare ground for a sleeping place is enough; a bowl of rice and a cup of the coffee he has learned to drink in foreign lands sufficient provender; but for those who honor his roof with their presence, he is bound by the law of Islam to provide more generous entertainment."

"Truly," returned Prasad, as his eyes wandered over the handsome furnishings of the house. "Truly if thou keepest all these things solely for the benefit of thy guests, thou must indeed be a prince of hospitality."

Ahmad consigned his friend to the care of a skillful barber, who, for an hour previous to the evening meal, deftly shaved, perfumed, and assisted in attiring the Hindu noble's person in garments befitting one to whom the Lord of the House desired to extend the greatest honor.

In order to avoid the least semblance of offense to his guest's susceptibilities, Ahmad had ordered the dishes of the repast to be prepared separately, those from which Prasad was to partake being cooked by a Brahman. For a similar reason water was served by one of that caste.

The meal was sumptuous, both in the display of gold and silver plate, and in the long succession of courses spiced to tempt the palate of an Oriental epicure.

Prasad's ill humor was plainly marked in his meagre appetite. Savory dishes, of which he would, under ordinary circumstances, have partaken with avidity, he barely tasted. Others, he let pass without even inserting his fingers to test their quality.

"Come," cried Ahmad, at the conclusion of the banquet, "thou shalt now drink of the choicest of the *Giours'* spirits. I warrant that after the first cup thy peace of mind will be restored. Thou wilt forget past disappointments in the happiness of the present."

Wine for Prasad's benefit, and coffee for the Mohammedan were then served. *Hookahs* were set before them and lit by obsequious servants.

Prasad cast restraint to the winds and drank deeply, while his companion watched him craftily, encouraging his libations. But the insidious spirits of the Foreigners, looted from their bungalows, only served to intensify his dejection.

"Accursed life," he muttered. "What am I, that I should submit so tamely to the fickle humor of the Rani"?

"Patience, good friend, a little patience," returned Ahmad assuagingly, yet with an added sting.

"Dost Ali is but a passing fancy. Forget him in the pleasure of the moment. Drink, and thou wilt surely feel a new man before the *Mollah's* voice at sunrise, calls the Faithful to their devotions."

He raised his hand as a signal to an attendant, a heavy curtain was drawn back and a group of musicians, accompanied by dancing girls arrayed in yards upon yards of silken drapery, entered the apartment. They advanced to the divan upon which the two nobles sat languidly drawing from their *hookahs* and *salaamed* deferentially. The musicians then seated themselves in a half circle in front of the divan, while the girls awaited the first bars from the instruments. Presently an inspiring air rose in the chamber, the girls assumed individual poses, and the *natch* commenced.

Their graceful actions, glancing steps, and sensuous attitudes, frequently called forth words of praise from the

Mohammedan; but Prasad's gloomy thoughts remained unconquered.

"Surely thou art hard to please," remarked Ahmad, as the girls retired for a brief rest.

"Thou knowest the distemper of my mind," replied the other sullenly.

"Aye, but wait," exclaimed Ahmad. "The jewel that shall bring fire into thine eyes hath not yet appeared."

He again gave a signal. The curtain was once more withdrawn. Upon the polished surface of a slab of ebony, uplifted upon the shoulders of six stalwart *harkars*, Ganga, the star of *natch* girls, was borne into the room.

For a moment, even Prasad's gaze rested approvingly upon the seductive form of the famous dancer. Her supple figure, attired in elaborately embroidered shawls, and colored silken skirts, artistically disclosed, one beneath another, was displayed with an effect well chosen to captivate those whom it was her profession to enthrall. Flowers adorned her hair. Her neck, arms, and ankles were ornamented with jeweled trinkets.

Upon the *harkars* halting before the divan, she raised her arms above her head, and assumed a graceful pose. In a low, fascinating tone, she commenced a dreamy song of love. Presently her feet caught the rhythm of the music, and to the accompaniment of tiny silver bells attached to the bangles on her wrists and ankles, she portrayed by her actions, in turn, the passions of love, hope, jealousy and despair.

From time to time Ahmad uttered exclamations of

"Didst thou mark that languorous glance she cast on thee?"—Page 105.

satisfaction. Prasad, in spite of himself seemed to be fascinated by her charm.

Ahmad quickly noticed his guest's brightening humor.

"What did I tell thee," he whispered insinuatingly. "Miserable indeed would be the man whose soul was insensible to the eyes of such a one. Didst thou mark that languorous glance she cast on thee"?

Prasad sighed heavily.

"I grant you," he replied, "with but one exception, she hath a matchless form. At any other time she might have made a fair impression. Now, chains bind my soul about a thankless vision."

The girl finished her part by lightly springing from her elevated position, and prostrating herself before the nobles.

Ahmad took from his waistband a handful of gold coins and tossed them to the girl.

"Take them, O Ganga," he cried. "By *Allah!* Thou hast almost performed a miracle. Thou hast found favor in the eye of the inconsolable."

A slight note of sarcasm marked the Mohammedan's concluding sentence.

Far into the night the two nobles watched the repeated efforts of the dancing girls, stimulated by cups of wine, to outdo their previous displays of art. But after the first surprise on beholding Ganga's charms, Prasad relapsed within his cloud of dejection.

At last, the early shafts of dawn penetrated the reed blinds and mingled their light with that of the silver lamps suspended from the roof; a warning that the moment of sunrise was at hand. Twittering of awakened birds, and the voices of men and beasts proclaimed for the multitude the passing of the hour from rest to labor.

Prasad rose wearily from his recumbent position.

"Ahmad," he exclaimed. "In truth, I feel as if I may be sick. Perchance thou wilt not be obliged to resort to subterfuge in my behalf."

Ahmad turned a penetrating look toward his guest.

"Thou wilt not attend the ceremony of to-day"? he asked.

"As thou advisest," returned the other. "Do what thou thinkest best for me. I am sick with love, with jealousy, with I know not what, for yonder Rani."

He turned and slowly made his way toward one of the exits from the room.

Ahmad also rose to a standing posture.

From the balcony of a minaret near by, the voice of a *Mollah* resounded through the clear atmosphere.

"There is but one God and Mohammed is the Prophet of God."

Ahmad strode from the room to a porch facing the west. He knelt and reverentially bowed his forehead to the pavement.

"Thanks be to God," he murmured devoutly, "for the countenance He turneth toward His servant."

Then he uplifted his face to the brightening heavens. He stretched forth his arms above his head, as he cried in a deep, sonorous voice:

"*Allah! Allah! Allah*"!

Chapter X

THE WHITE TURRET

IN the open space before the main entrance to the Rani's palace, a crowd of nobles, soldiers, and sightseers had collected. High mettled horses led by grooms, paced back and forth, while their owners in dazzling groups discussed the news of the morning. Peddlars of trifles, beggars, and ascetics, plied their various callings profitably in the interval awaiting the Rani's departure for the White Turret.

Before the door a suite of officers and servants in gala liveries, surrounded a royal elephant, gorgeously caparisoned with plumes, and scarlet velvet cloths embroidered with gold thread. To its back was strapped a canopied state *houdah* for the use of the Rani.

Near by, a groom with difficulty controlled the impatient spirit of a pure blue-black Arabian charger, the property of Ahmad Khan. The Mohammedan noble had entered the palace to make his daily report to the Rani.

Presently, without ceremony, the Rani came forth. A short period of confusion ensued as the nobles hurriedly sought their horses, and the soldiers pressed back the throng surging about the palace.

The Rani paused on the steps and gazed round as if she missed a familiar object. In so doing her eyes chanced to rest approvingly upon Ahmad's mount.

"Whose brave steed is that"? she asked of an attendant.

Ahmad strode forward and acknowledged himself as its owner.

"A gift from the Amir of Bukhara," he explained, "in recognition of a slight military service rendered. I prize the beast more than all the occupants of my stables together. No one hath ever crossed his back but myself, and," he added, "I doubt if anyone would care to try."

"Ah," laughed the Rani. "Dost wager a challenge then on Akbar's behalf"?

"Not I, fair Rani," returned the Mohammedan, "for it might mean a speedy death to one so venturesome."

Impulsively the Rani walked toward the beast. "Akbar," she cried, "Dost recognize a friend with those clear eyes of thine"?

The animal started, arched its proud neck, and snorted defiantly.

"Come, good Akbar," exclaimed the Rani soothingly. "Come. Thou art too noble a beast to display malice to a woman."

Fearlessly she raised her arm and affectionately stroked the glossy neck, passing her hand gently downward across its face.

A tremor passed over the beast's frame. It stamped the ground and whinnied as if half pleased with the caress, yet still uncertain in its humor.

Ahmad hurried to the Rani's side, while others watched with expressions of alarm.

"Noble Lady," he urged. "I pray thee touch not the beast. Its temper is so uncertain that I cannot answer for your safety."

The Rani again laughed lightly, as she permitted the animal to sniff her hair, her face, and hands.

"Ahbar knoweth whom to trust," she cried. "See, he discerneth a true Maratha, of whom it has been said, he is born in the saddle with a sword in his hand. I vow, O Ahmad," she added, "this day I will ride your Akbar, or go in no other manner to the White Turret."

Before Ahmad could interpose a further objection, she had gathered the reins in her hand, placed her foot in the stirrup, and sprung lightly on to the charger's back.

The horse swerved violently, then halted, with ears set back and form rigid.

A moment of suspense for those watching followed.

"Come Akbar," urged the Rani firmly, while gently patting the beast's neck. "Come, thou must curb thy temper for thou canst not throw a daughter of the Marathas."

The beast pricked up its ears at her voice, and neighed its subjection.

"Ah, Ahmad," she cried with taunting pleasantry, "thou must seek another mount. Why not ride in the *howdah* of my elephant. How much didst thou wager, friend"?

"Surely the devil is in the girl," he muttered in astonished accents. "What will be her next performance"?

A servant approached the Rani deferentially.

"If my Lady Rani," said he, "elects to ride on horseback, will she let her pleasure be known concerning the noble elephant"?

"Truly," she replied. "If Ahmad Khan likes not to go in so much state, let my worthy secretary, Bipin Dat mount on high. From that exalted perch, he can survey the heavens and the earth complacently, frown majestically upon the populace, and imagine that he has at last become a Maharaja."

The Rani shook the reins and curveted to the front of her nobles.

Gallantly she led the brilliant cavalcade through the bazaars and streets to that part of the walls upon which the White Turret had been specially erected to fly her banner.

Plaudits saluted her progress on all sides. The people were accustomed to witness the exercise of greater personal freedom on the part of the Maratha ladies, to what is usually accorded women of high rank in other parts of India, but it was the first time they had beheld a princess of such beauty and high spirit leading, instead of being surrounded by the retinue of her court.

With admirable skill she controlled Ahmad's restive charger, until shortly, as if proud of its lovely burden, the beast followed obediently the guidance of her hand. At the bastion of the White Turret she dismounted and approached the spot where a group of officers awaited her arrival.

Her banner was already bent to the halliards, and held

by a lieutenant so that its silken folds might not be sullied by contact with the ground. Near by, a soldier stood at a gun ready to ignite the powder of a first salute as the flag rose upon its staff.

The nobles grouped themselves about the Rani. An officer holding the halliards begged to know her command.

For a moment she hesitated. Then as if a sudden impulse had taken possession of her mind, she took the ropes from his hand and turned toward the nobles.

"My Lords," she cried. "The Rani will herself raise her banner on the walls of Jhansi, aye, and defend it, against whatsoever enemy may come."

Slowly hand upon hand she pulled upon the rope. Slowly the banner, embroidered with her device, rose upon the staff. It reached the top and waved proudly in a gentle breeze against the pale blue morning sky. A white cloud of smoke for an instant hung over the ditch below the bastion, as the tongue of the cannon saluted her military rank. Spontaneously swords flashed in the bright sunlight: spontaneously a loud chorus rose, mingled with the repeated roar of the cannon, hailing the fair defender of a throne.

"Lachmi Bai! Lachmi Bai! Rani of Jhansi," they cried.

She gazed round with joyful gratitude. A moment later, the same wistful look that marked her countenance upon the palace steps, came back into her eyes.

She beckoned Ahmad to her side.

"Where is the noble Prasad Singh"? she asked. "I have not seen him since the *Darbar* of yesterday."

An expression of regret settled upon Ahmad's face.

"Noble Rani," he explained. "Prasad Singh is sick."

His manner and intonation, whether intentional or otherwise, clearly implied a desire to conceal another reason.

The Rani returned his gaze penetratingly.

"I would speak with thee upon our return to the palace," she enjoined.

Ahmad bowed his compliance to her wish.

The ceremony was over. The Rani thanked the nobles for their renewed demonstration of affection. She again urged them to lose no time in repairing the defenses of their fortresses, and in the arming and drilling of fresh troops. She bade them farewell until she would again summon them to *Darbar*.

So while the Rani's banner fluttered defiantly from the peak of the White Turret, the procession retraced its way to the palace. Upon the Rani's countenance happiness called forth by the enthusiastic greetings of the people, was occasionally shaded by a look of disappointment. Something evidently had been wanting to complete the gladness of the hour.

On dismounting she summoned Ahmad to follow her into the interior.

"My Lord," she said, when they were alone, "thy reply concerning Prasad Singh causeth me to suspect that something hath gone amiss with him. Hath the foolish fellow taken umbrage at some new imaginary slight"?

Ahmad looked uneasy. He hesitated to reply, as if under the necessity of exercising prudent dissimulation.

"Thou dost not answer me," resumed the Rani, in a tone of some impatience. "Tell me, I command thee, why it was that Prasad Singh did not comply with my invitation to be present at the ceremony of the morning"?

"Fair Lady," Ahmad replied evasively, "surely the truth is, that the noble Prasad Singh is sick. I doubt not he was unable to be present."

"Sick is he," the Rani echoed, "Aye, but thy manner leadeth me to suspect another cause. I beg thee, good Ahmad, to tell me the nature of his malady. Is it a distemper of the mind"?

"Noble Rani," returned Ahmad, "Prasad Singh is sick. I ask thee to urge me to no further explanation."

"But I will urge thee," retorted the Rani imperiously. "I will have the whole truth from thee ere thou dost leave the palace."

Ahmad Khan appeared a victim of deep confusion.

"Most gracious Rani," he besought her, "I trust thou wilt not visit thy displeasure upon one who is my friend, my good comrade. Verily do I love Prasad as a brother. Ill would it seem in me to expose the pardonable follies of a gallant youth."

"Follies," exclaimed the Rani petulantly. "Speak! What follies hath Prasad Singh committed"?

Ahmad assumed an apologetic mien.

"Merely, noble lady," he replied, "the usual overflow of spirit in one of his high birth. He hath indulged too freely of the accursed spirits of the Foreigners."

A look of disdain settled on the Rani's face.

"So," she cried. "Like too many others he forgets the precepts of his caste. This, I did not think of Prasad. The spirits of the Foreigners! Truly one of the many curses brought to India in their civilizing wake." She concluded with intense bitterness in her voice.

"Noble Rani," continued Ahmad. "It was to draw him from the evil habit that I took him to my house; but alas! by some means he procured the *Giours'* intoxicating drink, and—"

He checked himself suddenly as if he would draw back from disclosing a moral precipice yawning beneath Prasad's life.

"And," caught up the Rani quickly. "And what more, good Ahmad Khan. What more hast thou to tell of Prasad"?

"Noble Rani," he petitioned with apparent earnestness. "I implore thee now to close my mouth."

"Nay, thou shalt open it the wider," she rejoined. "Speak, tell all thou knowest, I command thee."

"Miserable, faithless friend, that I must appear," he exclaimed self reproachfully.

"Thou wouldst be a disloyal servant if thou didst not obey thy Rani," she retorted. "Come! It is the Rani who commands thee."

He spoke in a tone of regretful emotion.

"Thou hast heard, noble Rani, of the charms of a certain *natch* girl, Ganga, by name"? he asked.

"Aye," she replied tersely.

"Alas! then," continued Ahmad. "The noble Prasad lyeth sick or drunk, I know not which, of the *Giours'* spirits and the subtle influence of this dancer of Kashmir."

For a moment even Ahmad quailed before the display of jealous anger on the Rani's face. She raised her arm with a threatening gesture as if about to give full play to her resentment; but as suddenly as the flame of passion had been called forth, as quickly it yielded to her control of temperament.

"Go," she commanded in a quiet voice, made more impressive by the emotion with difficulty suppressed. "Go, tell Prasad Singh, the Rani orders his presence hither immediately. If he delays, he may mount his horse and ride forth from her state.

"I have spoken," she concluded, turning from the Mohammedan.

"Noble Lady," petitioned Ahmad, "thou dost not blame thy servant for disclosing that which his conscience had enjoined him to conceal. Alas! Prasad hath eaten of Ahmad's salt."

"Thou hast obeyed my command," she replied. "In so doing thou didst well."

Ahmad bowed low and left the apartment.

The Rani turned again to watch his retreating form. When it had disappeared from view, sorrowfully she unfettered her emotion.

"Oh! that Prasad—Prasad, whom as a woman I have loved, and as the Rani I would honor, should appear in such a weak, a worthless light. Prasad, my Prasad," she cried, "that thou of all men shouldst be the shadow to darken my hour of happiness.

A sob broke from her lips. She covered her face with her hands.

Chapter XI

A SHREWD DIAGNOSIS

IN spite of the Rani's urgent dispatch, Ahmad returned leisurely to his house. If gravity rested on his face, his spirit was grimly elated at the successful progress of his design upon Prasad.

"The accursed Hindu," he muttered at intervals. "He is well enmeshed in the net God has placed in the hands of His humble servant."

Prasad expectantly awaited his host's arrival on the porch. He marked the Mohammedan's serious aspect and begged of him the reason.

"Hath something gone amiss, good friend"? he asked anxiously.

Ahmad waved his hand indifferently, as he drew Prasad to a room apart.

"It is nothing that can be defined clearly," he returned, "but a feeling of uneasiness caused by the Rani's capricious humor. One knows not what to expect of her next. At the ceremony of the morning she first insisted upon riding to the White Turret on my Arabian charger, Akbar; and then raised her banner with her own hands. In truth, though," he cried with a note of genuine admiration, "I cannot but own she made a brave display of spirit. She looked as gallant a captain as ever rode at the head of a troop. The people worship her, the nobles prostrate themselves at her feet, even Akbar, who never yet submitted to the caress of any mortal being, acted like a lover at the sound of her voice, and followed the guidance of her hand as obediently as a faithful hound. I confess I know not what to make of her."

"True, O Ahmad," acquiesced Prasad. "Thou hast in part stated my own sentiment in regard to her. I know not what to make of the peerless Rani. But tell me," he urged, "did she notice my absence? Did she by word or sign indicate her feeling"?

Ahmad replied thoughtfully.

"I make no doubt the Rani marked thy absence, O Prasad, for it seems nothing of any moment escapes her notice. But as she loveth thee, she is far too circumspect a woman to disclose her tender sentiment in public. A favor she may cast here and there, as in the case of this Dost Ali; but the expression of her deeper feeling she will keep for thy ear alone. Thou wilt doubtless hear from her in some covert manner. She will, in turn, upbraid thee for thy negligence, and lavish upon thee tributes of her devotion. Have patience, good friend, for it is no boast that Ahmad Khan hath not mingled in more than one court intrigue without learning somewhat of the devious ways of women. Thou must control thy passion for a little."

"Patience"! exclaimed the other with every sign of impatience. "How can I have patience when I think she may, even at this moment, be casting her ravishing smiles upon Dost Ali."

"Ah! Dost Ali," Ahmad returned contemptuously. "Think not of him. He is but a feather wafted to her feet to-day, and to-morrow blown by the wind of Fate, God alone knows whither."

Prasad cast himself wearily upon a divan.

"Ahmad," he exclaimed. "Verily am I sick. I know not what it is that ails me."

Ahmad regarded his guest with apparent concern.

"Aye," he responded, "thou dost look unwell. Thy brow is feverish. Thou art out of humor, and hadst better see a skilful physician who will soon set thee in order. One such as I have in mind, the worthy doctor and astrologer, Mohurran Goshi. He hath mastered all the ancient schools of medicine; a man of profound learning, a sure foreteller of things about to happen."

"I beg thou wouldst send for him quickly," besought Prasad, "that he may relieve me of the burden that seems to be crushing me to earth."

Ahmad readily complied. He summoned an attendant, by whom he dispatched an urgent call to the astrologer.

In the meantime he regaled Prasad with the gossip of the court. He told of the ceremony at the White Turret, referring insinuatingly to the favor displayed toward Dost Ali, and of the Rani's varying humor.

As a consequence Prasad's restlessness and jealousy increased, in spite of the mollifying clause which Ahmad invariably subjoined.

The jolting of a bullock cart as it rumbled along the

uneven road leading up to Ahmad's door, told of the astrologer's arrival.

Ahmad went forth to meet him alone. As soon as the astrologer had alighted, the Mohammedan engaged him in a whispered conversation.

"Thou fully understandeth thy part, learned Astrologer," he said in conclusion.

"Most rightly, noble Lord," the other answered obsequiously.

"Thy reward shall be greater than even thy mind can conjure, if thou art successful in ridding Jhansi of this meddlesome interloper," Ahmad promised. He conducted the astrologer-physician to Prasad's side.

In a bag slung over one shoulder, Mohurran Goshi carried his medicinal pills and ointments; while in the hand of the other arm, he grasped his calendar, and certain instruments pertaining to the occult branch of his dual profession. He approached Prasad and felt the patient's pulse gravely. Gravely, too, he examined Prasad's tongue, shook his head several times significantly, and then betook himself to a seat on the floor near by, where he absorbed his mind in a deep scrutiny of his calendar, intermittently muttering an unintelligible jargon.

As a result he finally delivered a sage diagnosis of the case.

"It is clear, noble sir," he said, addressing Prasad, "that the origin of your malady lies in the evil influence of an enemy working through the affection of one upon whom your heart is set, but whose notice he has temporarily beguiled. Most fortunate is it that you have called to your assistance, in time, a physician-astrologer, by profound study and long experience, well fitted to combat such designs."

Mohurran Goshi glanced craftily toward Ahmad, and gleaning that thus far his opinion was being well received, proceeded:

"By a sure sign I can demonstrate to you, great sir, the truth of what I affirm, that I am able to avert impending misfortune on your behalf, restore the object of your affection to your arms, and further you in your ambition. Soon will your sickness pass away like darkness before the rising sun. Is it the noble Lord's pleasure that I should do this"?

Prasad had not escaped the atmosphere of superstition in which the majority of his race had from time unknown been reared. In his condition of mind he was more than ready to fall a victim to the wiles of the astrologer.

"Do so," he replied. "From what you have said I feel great confidence in your ability."

The astrologer first called for a bowl of water in which he requested Prasad to wash his hands and forearms. Then he produced a splinter of bone which he required his patient to hold in the water, while he muttered in a low tone for several minutes.

The incantation over, he bade Prasad withdraw his hand from the water, when there appeared, a little above the wrist, the blotch of a human form impressed upon the skin by some dark stain.

The astrologer pointed to the mark on Prasad's arm with triumph.

"Behold, my Lord," he cried, "the image of thine enemy, the one who seeks to do thee so much injury."

Both Ahmad and Prasad expressed their astonishment at what appeared to them a miraculous display of the astrologer's skill.

"Now, my Lord," resumed Mohurran Goshi. "If it be thy pleasure that I should foil this enemy of thine, thou hast but to give thy command."

Prasad well understood the covert allusion to a fee in advance implied by the astrologer, and produced a handful of silver coins to secure his valuable services.

These, the astrologer tucked safely away on his person, and then proceeded to destroy the malign influence aiming for his patient's ruin.

From Prasad's hand he took the bone, and smeared it with an ointment, which he declared was composed of the most precious ingredients—the fat of a cobra, the blood of a white rat, salt, and the hoof of an animal unknown to them. He then rubbed the blotch on Prasad's arm with the bone for a space, again muttering unintelligibly, when lo! the image had disappeared.

The astrologer solemnly held up the bone before his patient's eyes.

"Into this, noble sir, have I gathered the influence which causes you so much bodily and mental anguish."

With wonder, the eyes of the two nobles gazed upon the bone fraught with so much magic charm. Though as a Mohammedan, Ahmad affected to scoff at the mysterious science professed by the astrologer, his hereditary instinct at times caused him momentary qualms, when inexplicable demonstrations of its power were afforded.

The astrologer next called for a metal tray, a seed, and a gold coin. These produced, he placed the seed, the gold coin, and the piece of bone together on the tray, and once more solemnly muttered incantations over them. As Ahmad and Prasad watched intently, in a twinkling the bone leaped into the air and disappeared.

"Thus, my Lord," cried Mohurran Goshi, "will thy trouble depart from thee, if thou art careful to follow my directions.

Prasad breathed a deep sigh of relief as if already a great weight had been lifted from his mind.

The astrologer then took the coin and passed it several times over his patient's head, muttering incantations as before, and finally inserted it in a fold of Prasad's turban. In the process it strangely changed from the precious metal into copper, another convincing proof of the astrologer's extraordinary power over inanimate things.

He then took the seed, and wrapping it in a sheet of paper bearing cabalistic signs, handed it to Prasad.

"This," said he, "is to place beneath your pillow, which, with the coin, will surely ward off a return of the evil influence. Now as to the medicine for your body."

From his bag he drew forth several pills, compounded, he asserted, of ground pearls, coral, and an herb of wonderful medicinal virtue, only found with difficulty in the high altitudes of the Himalayas. These he enjoined Prasad to take at certain intervals, setting a price upon them that might have warranted their curative power over any ill to which mortal flesh is heir.

"Now," said he, "it will be well for you not to leave the illustrious Ahmad Khan's roof for some days, during which I will call to mark your progress, but," he added insinuatingly, "if through the medium of a discreet friend, the object of your affection could be brought to your side, there is no doubt you would attain a speedy recovery. A slight cloud is still suspended over your head, but with my aid, be assured, it will be dispelled at the fitting moment."

Mohurran Goshi then gave some directions regarding the patient's food, gathered his effects together, consigned the two nobles to the protection of God, *salaamed* several times before them, and went forth to climb into his rickety bullock cart.

"A sage and skilful physician," remarked Ahmad approvingly.

"Undoubtedly," coincided Pasad. "Now that he hath assured me that the accursed Dost Ali will be removed from my path, I feel a change for the better."

"Did I not assure thee that with patience all would come well," rejoined Ahmad.

"Aye, truly, good friend; but didst thou remark the last advice of the learned physician"? asked Prasad.

"Regarding the mission of a discreet friend"? queried Ahmad in return.

"To be sure."

"That is an easy matter," exclaimed Ahmad reassuringly. "To-morrow when I make my report to the Rani I can prudently disclose to her thy unhappy condition. No one, good Prasad, can for a purpose assume a more sympathetic tone of voice, or a more pleading expression, than thy friend the man of arms. In a moment, I warrant, the fair Rani will be at thy side."

"Do this for me," returned Prasid in a grateful voice, "and there is nothing thou canst not ask of me."

Ahmad vowed solemnly that it would be his chief duty on the morrow.

"And now," said he. "If thou art ordered a meagre diet, the learned astrologer-physician said nothing against a bountiful feast for the eyes. Let us see what the fair Ganga can do to assist us in passing a leisure hour."

"As thou wilt," returned Prasad, evincing but little interest in his host's suggestion. "Ganga is well enough doubtless for one whose soul is not captivated by an incomparable form."

Ahmad glanced with the suggestion of a smile toward his guest.

"The swine," he muttered underneath his breath.

Chapter XII

AHMAD AGAIN NONPLUSSED

IN the furtherance of his design, Ahmad anticipated what might be termed a scene when he made his report to the Rani upon the following morning. He fully expected, from his observation of the character of women in general, that he would find her enraged and vindictive with Prasad, as the result of the Hindu noble's failure to respond promptly to her summons. In this respect he was again destined to experience a surprise, if not a disappointment.

She received him sedately as became the nature of the business to be transacted, and without a reference to the event which had caused her to display so much feeling on the day before. If Prasad's image still occupied a place in her mind, no mention of his name came from her lips to mark her sentiment toward him. Had her heart been entirely free from the tender passion, she could not have appeared more composed, more secure in all that related to her nature as a woman.

From time to time Ahmad gazed upon her with wonder. In order to draw forth from her an outburst of the fire of resentment which he was convinced burned inwardly, he more than once skillfully turned the conversation in the direction of her truant lover; but the Rani as skillfully declined his lead, passing on naturally to matters of public importance.

She absolutely refused to disclose, from the beginning to the end of the interview, what her thoughts or intentions were in regard to the Mohammedan's rival.

As he was about to leave her presence, Ahmad paused on the threshold with the hope that she would yet make some reference to Prasad.

The Rani glanced toward him interrogatively.

"Hast thou more to say, O Ahmad"? she asked calmly.

"Nothing, nothing, great Lady," he answered falteringly, as he saluted.

She returned the salute with dignity.

"Then I wish thee good fortune until the morrow," she concluded.

He left the palace with uneasy speculations rising in his mind. Treacherous to the core of his nature himself, the Rani's reserve of manner, caused him to suspect that treachery was lurking somewhere among his own following.

Could that rascal of an astrologer be playing a double part? was the first thought that flashed into Ahmad's brain; or could Prasad be acting in the Rani's confidence as a spy upon his actions? If the latter happened to be the case, he reasoned that the Hindu noble must possess a power of deception of which he had certainly not displayed the least symptom as yet. Ahmad decided that this was unlikely. If, then, the astrologer was in reality conspiring against him, for greater pay on the part of someone else, a possible enough contingency, it could easily be detected. In any case he perceived the necessity of bringing Prasad's complete ruin in the Rani's estimation to a speedy issue, or a chance disclosure of his intrigue might engulf him hopelessly in the ditch, he had so well excavated for his rival.

He set spurs to his horse and rode quickly to the astrologer's house.

A prolonged conversation with Mohurran Goshi apparently satisfied Ahmad that he had nothing to fear from the duplicity of that crafty personage. He handed the astrologer a well filled purse as the best tonic to stimulate his continued fidelity.

"Thou wilt call, then, to see thy patient later in the day, learned Astrologer," Ahmad remarked, as he prepared to turn his face homeward.

"At thy command, noble Lord," acquiesced the astrologer submissively.

"It is well," exclaimed Ahmad. "I warrant thou wilt find him in an excellent humor for thy purpose."

Ahmad tested the speed of his horse until he approached within a short distance of the compound surrounding his dwelling. Then he slackened his pace and assumed an air of grave dejection.

"Good Prasad must believe that the heart of Ahmad Khan goes out to him in sympathy," he soliloquized, "while the disclosure of the Rani's faithlessness is drawn forth unwillingly from his friendly lips."

Prasad awaited the Mohammedan's return in a state

of feverish anxiety. He remarked Ahmad's gloomy visage immediately.

"Thou art the bearer of ill news, O Ahmad," he exclaimed, ere the usual greetings had been exchanged.

"Alas"! returned the other. "My countenance doubtless reflects the sadness of my heart."

"Speak," enjoined Prasad. "Tell me the worst thou knowest, for I feel assured it hath to deal with my unlucky case."

"The worst may be told quickly enough, good friend," replied Ahmad. "Yet, I would that thou urgest me not to such an unpleasant office. Let us discuss other matters, and leave the disagreeable topic to a later hour."

Prasad waved his hand impatiently.

"Tell me quickly," he cried. "Bad news is like decaying fruit. It becomes the more rotten with the keeping. Did the Rani refuse to hearken to my request"?

"Aye, she did even more than that," came the reply. "She refused to have thy name mentioned in her presence."

"So"! ejaculated Prasad. "What else hast thou to tell, my emissary"?

"Why, good Prasad, as I hold thy interest at heart it pains me deeply to speak thus, but it doth seem the Rani hath cast herself body and soul into the arms of this new favorite, Dost Ali. Her actions have become the scandal of the court."

Prasad raised himself upon his elbow. His brow contracted and his eyes flashed threateningly.

"Tell me more," he hoarsely muttered.

"In truth, there is little more to tell," rejoined Ahmad, "except, that she rides, walks, and feasts with him, and, the court gossip saith, yields somewhat more besides. As for me, my business over, she excused my presence speedily. I would have kept this from thee, but rumor would surely have broken through my desire."

Prasad rose and paced back and forth in ominous silence. Suddenly he turned and spoke vehemently.

"Ahmad, sick or well, I vow I will not be supplanted by this Dost Ali. Immediately will I go to the palace. Toward the Rani I mean no harm, but with her lover, I will find an excuse to bring this matter to an end between us. Either Prasad Singh or Dost Ali shall fall into the dust."

Ahmad laid a restraining hand upon the Hindu noble's shoulder.

"Prasad," he enjoined, "thou canst not do this."

"Why should I not"? the other asked tersely.

"Because there must be no strife within the Rani's palace. It would be an act against her pleasure, her authority. Deeply do I sympathize with thee, O Prasad, but I cannot countenance thy project."

Prasad returned his host's gaze with astonishment.

"Then, in heaven's name, what wouldst thou have me do"? he demanded. "Lie here like some decrepit hunter while another goes off with the quarry. Not I forsooth"!

"Come, good friend, curb thy ambition, passion, and

impetuosity for a season. Await with patience the fitting opportunity for achieving all, without resort to violent means, that would implacably offend the Rani. Thou must remember her palace is not a camp, a field of arms."

"Oh"! exclaimed Prasad sarcastically. "These are indeed strange words from Ahmad Khan. Is it so long ago that he and his followers swept into her palace little heeding her authority. Truly that scene resembled an assault."

Ahmad winced at the retort but managed to preserve his equanimity. He replied in a contrite tone.

"It is even as thou sayest, but the hour was full of tumult. If my action seemed wanting in respect for the Rani's dignity, surely I have made the amends I swore upon the holy book."

Prasad laughed cynically.

"Loyal Ahmad," he cried. "I see not very well how thou canst prevent me settling with this Dost Ali."

"What I will prevent," the Mohammedan answered, as if conscious of a virtuous motive, "is the hasty action of a friend leading him on to certain ruin, aye, even if I surround the house with soldiers and hold him as a prisoner. Prasad, the Rani in her present temper would never forgive thee. Thou must, nay thou shalt have patience, for thine own interest. Even if thou dost curse thy friend now, he knows thou wilt presently call down blessings on his head."

The two regarded each other fixedly. On Ahmad's

face, entreaty that gave place to determination. Prasad's countenance, a display of conflicting emotions.

"Come," resumed Ahmad soothingly. "Subdue thy resentment. I tell thee thy trouble will pass over, and thou wilt find thyself high in favor with the Rani. In the meantime enjoy thy enforced absence from her court as becomes a noble of high spirit. Drink of the Foreigner's spirits, and," he added in a lower tone, "if thou wilt, of the charms of the fair Ganga. There are hundreds who would envy thy present opportunity."

"A curse upon all this mischief," Prasad returned impatiently.

"Hath not the learned astrologer told thee all will come well"? asked the Mohammedan reassuringly.

"A curse upon him, too," added Prasad. "If he observed a little more carefully events passing on the earth instead of keeping his gaze fixed upon the heavens, he would be able to prophesy more surely. The fool! Were I the Raja of Jhansi, I would soon find a means to make him lament his fate, for having disclosed such a budget of nonsense."

"Thou knowest that as a follower of the only true Prophet," replied Ahmad. "I set little store upon his trade as an astrologer; but as a physician, he hath a reputation whereby he is sought by the greatest nobles and princes."

"I care not for him or his reputation," returned Prasad sullenly. "To me, it seems, as if all men, aye and all women, are leagued against me."

"That is because thou art sick. Wait a day or two and thou wilt see things more reasonably. Because for the moment the flower thou longest to possess lies a little beyond thy reach, content thyself with others that are near to hand. Now I go to the cantonments to inspect the troops. When I return we will together discuss a means of getting rid of this Dost Ali without offending against the susceptibilities of the Rani; for in that, upon the oath that I have made, I can take no part."

With a further profession of his unalterable friendship, Ahmad departed to his military duties.

He had gone but an hour or so, a period consumed by Prasad in bitter reflections and vows of revenge upon his supposed rival, when the bullock cart of the astrologer again rumbled and creaked its slow progress to the Mohammedan's door.

Prasad received him in illhumored silence.

The astrologer-physician nevertheless methodically proceeded to unpack his bag, and to an examination of his patient.

As before, he gravely felt Prasad's pulse, observed his tongue, and then expressed himself as being highly satisfied with the sick man's improved condition.

"I had purposed advising thee to take a bath of oil," said he, "but I find it will be unnecessary."

"Truly thou art a wise physician," remarked Prasad sarcastically. "Tell me now, I beg, how the heavens look this evening for the attainment of my wishes"?

The astrologer scrutinized his calendar for a space, then replied in a satisfied tone.

"All goes well, noble sir. The moment of triumph over thine enemy draws nigh. She whom thou lovest will fly to thy arms speedily."

"Now of all the nonsense uttered by man, thou art talking the uttermost," replied Prasad in angry accents. "Dost know, learned Astrologer, that only this morning, after all that gibberish of thine yesterday, I heard the worst news possible"?

The astrologer instead of displaying offense at such a disparaging summary of his ability, appeared to expect the news.

"Noble sir," he argued in response. "That is as I anticipated. It often happens that a clearing sky is preceded by a thunderstorm. If thou wilt but hold thy patience for two days, then the moment for a determined action will have come."

"How do you mean"? asked Prasad doubtfully.

"Noble Lord," continued the astrologer in a confidential manner. "First I must have thy assurance that thou wilt not disclose a word of what I am about to unfold to thy illustrious host, Ahmad Khan.

"In truth he is thy friend, but in the enterprise which it will be well for thee to undertake, he will render thee no assistance, on account of a certain oath he has taken."

Prasad appeared to resume an interest in the astrologer's words.

" Proceed quickly," he urged. " Thou hast my promise."

" Then great sir," continued the astrologer. " Be pleased to know, that the fair one with whom thou art enamored, lies under the influence of one from whom she would gladly be delivered. If thou wert to repair to her side accompanied by a few trustworthy followers, at a favorable hour, she would hail thy appearance with joy, and thou couldst subdue thine enemy with ease."

" Come, learned Astrologer," interposed Prasad, his humor brightening perceptibly. " Now I realize thou art a man of action, and consequently a man of sense. Speak more plainly how thou wouldst advise. Be assured thou wilt be rewarded relatively with my success."

" Little further is there to say, noble Singh," returned the astrologer," except that the signs in the heavens declare midnight two days from hence to be the auspicious moment."

Prasad thought deeply for some minutes. At last he again spoke:

" Secluded here as I am, sage Doctor, it would be difficult for me to arrange the plan of action. I would that you suggest one for me."

The astrologer glanced round suspiciously as if to note that they were not overheard.

" That is an easy matter, noble Lord," he replied. " If thou wilt keep in mind my injunction not to breathe a word of it to Ahmad Khan, and repair to the tomb of

Firoz Khan, nigh the temple of Siva, overlooking the lake at one hour before midnight, I will arrange to have two or three good fellows to meet thee there. A greater number would arouse suspicion at the gate, but for thy purpose they will be sufficient. The palace will be asleep, and thine enemy taken off his guard."

"Thou seemest to know well the secrets of this affair, learned Astrologer," remarked Prasad.

"Such is my profession, noble sir," replied Mohurran Goshi, with a note of pride in his voice.

Prasad again buried himself in thought before he spoke.

"Yes, learned Doctor," he rejoined finally. "If thou art sure thou canst aid me in the way suggested, I have more than made up my mind to follow thy counsel."

A momentary flicker of satisfaction crossed the astrologer's crafty face.

"As certain, noble sir," he replied emphatically, "as that the sand in the hour glass of thine enemy's fortune hath all but emptied itself into the lower vessel."

"Then I will be there," decided Prasad, "at the appointed place and hour."

"Good, noble Lord," exclaimed the astrologer. "Be assured I, too, will keep my part of the agreement. Hast thou taken the medicinal pills regularly"? he asked with professional concern.

"To the devil with all pills and ointments," retorted Prasad. "My stomach yearns for other diet."

"Nevertheless, sir," enjoined the astrologer in his

character of physician. "They possess among other virtues that of stimulating the heart with courage."

"I want no such stimulants," retorted Prasad. "An enchanting form ever present in my mind is stimulant enough for any act requiring courage. If they would only assist me in controlling my impatience for the hour to come, then I might regard them as of some benefit."

"That they will also do, noble sir," asserted the astrologer. "Their extraordinary value lies in the fact that they are beneficial for any bodily or mental ailment."

"Then they must be as remarkable in virtue as they are in price," returned Prasad tersely.

He took a jewel from his turban and handed it to the astrologer.

"This," said he, "is but a small portion of the reward I will bestow upon thee, if thy plan turns out as well as it promises."

The astrologer expressed his gratitude in effusive terms.

"But be careful that not even the walls shall hear of it"? he enjoined.

"Fear not," replied Prasad. "At an hour before midnight I will be at the tomb of Firoz Khan on the day after to-morrow. See to it that the men are awaiting me."

"Without fail, noble sir," reasserted the astrologer.

He solemnly called down a thousand benedictions upon

Prasad's head, *salaamed,* and with an air of profound mystery, retired to seek his bullock cart.

"Now," ejaculated Prasad triumphantly. "We will see how this Dost Ali can be brought to an accounting in spite of Ahmad's qualms of conscience."

He called for a goblet of the Foreigners' wine, and drank with evident appreciation of its quality.

Chapter XIII

WHAT BIPIN OVERHEARD

BIPIN DAT was returning from his morning prayers at the temple of Vishnu absorbed in thought. His brow was puckered, his eyes directed toward the ground, as he made his way slowly through the press in the bazaar. In his mind serious doubt had arisen regarding the power of the good tempered God of the great middle caste to avert the calamity which the astrologer persistently reasserted was suspended over his head. Manifestly, it was useless, he reasoned, to continue his offerings at the shrine of a deity, who either could or would not protect him, when the face of some other of the innumerable personages of the Hindu pantheon was turned with vindictive anger upon his career. The difficulty was to discover the God to be propitiated, as by an unlucky chance he might overlook the very one causing him so much unhappiness. Truly it was a perplexing situation for the worthy secretary. He almost wished he were a Mohammedan with only one God from which to choose.

With unbounded pride ever directing his vision to impossible heights, he had come to believe that eventually he might forsake the God of his birth and assume the right to pay tribute to Siva the mystical God of the Brahmans; but clearly this was not the hour for the worship of a deity enveloped in an abstract philosophy. A man with his ears and nose, if not his life, in momentary danger is inclined to resort to a more tangible incarnation of divine power, and possibly wrath. With terror enthroned in his soul, what more human than that he should turn to Siva in that deity's non-Aryan form, as the awe inspiring God of the mass of the people, or his wife the bloody fury, the serpent crowned Kali. On the morrow he determined to prostrate himself covertly in the temple of the third person of the great Hindu Triad, and see if a better result might not be obtained. He heartily wished he was within reasonable distance of a shrine of holy Mother Ganges, for assuredly immersion in the waters of the sacred river, could not fail to appease all the Gods, by this one supreme act of devotion.

So deeply absorbed was Bipin in this all important problem, that he had failed to more than casually notice the actions of a small boy with well fattened limbs, displayed to somewhat unnecessary advantage by a string tied round his waist with a charm attached as his sole approach to clothing.

At every few steps taken by the secretary, the small boy ran forward and interposing his chubby form, *salaamed* respectfully.

Several times Bipin had stepped to one side under the impression that the boy's intention was merely to show respect for one of such exalted station, but at last becoming conscious of the youngster's persistency, Bipin halted and frowned down upon him threateningly.

"How now, boy"? he asked sternly. "What do you mean by continually getting in my way"?

"Great Secretary Sahib," replied the boy. "I am the son of Mohurran Goshi."

"*Wah*"! exclaimed Bipin. "So you are the son of Mohurran Goshi. Well! what does the son of Mohurran Goshi mean by repeatedly making of himself a stumbling block for my feet"?

"Lord Protector of the Poor," replied the boy deferentially. "My father bade me seek thee urgently with the message that thou art to repair to his house, without fail, two hours after sunset."

"Thy father bade thee tell me that I am to come to his house two hours after sunset," repeated Bipin reflectively. "Did he say for what purpose, dutiful son of Mohurran Goshi"?

"Not he, great sir," replied the boy, *salaaming*.

Bipin thought for a moment. It was possible that the astrologer had discovered a charm that would forever confound the machinations of the accursed Hindu noble.

"What answer shall I take from the great Secretary Raja"? asked the boy with a twinkle of innate cunning.

Bipin gazed approvingly on the lad who flattered his vanity by the use of such high sounding titles.

"Thou art a well favored youth," he remarked, "and properly trained in the respect due to people of importance. Go, tell thy learned father, that I will be at his door at the hour appointed."

As Bipin took a step forward the boy again interposed his person with outstretched hand.

"A present, Secretary Raja," he cried. "A present."

"Ah, a present," returned the secretary. "What now do you want with a present"?

"To buy sweetmeats, noble Lord," the boy answered.

Bipin discovered a small coin in his waist-band, and gave it to the astrologer's son.

The boy *salaamed* his thanks, and danced off to a nearby stall, making a sly grimace at the vanishing back of the Rani's worthy secretary.

A little before the time set by the astrologer, Bipin urged a matter of importance as an excuse for his absence from the palace, and directed his steps toward Mohurran Goshi's humble abode.

He found the astrologer in a state of suppressed excitement.

"There is not a moment to lose, worthy Secretary," said he. "Shortly thou wilt be in possession of information that will enable thee to frustrate thine enemy for all time. With it, thou canst repair to the Rani and ask any reward at her hands. But be careful not to disclose the source of thy information, or thou wilt surely fail in thy object. Come, follow quickly, and hold thy peace at whatever thou mayest see or hear, or our lives would go out as a torch flung into a pond."

Mohurran Goshi rapidly led the Rani's secretary by dark, narrow alleys, to one of the gates of the city, and thence out a short distance along a by-path to a small hut secluded amid a clump of trees. The absence of a light and the usual yelping of mongrel dogs, suggested the inference that the place was, at least, temporarily uninhabited. Mohurran Goshi again enjoined the strictest silence upon Bipin and bade him remain in the shadow of an out-building, while he went forward apparently to reconnoiter. Bipin watched his guide approach the door cautiously and listen. In a few minutes the astrologer returned stealthily, and beckoned Bipin to follow. He led Bipin round to the rear of the house and halted beside an open window. From within two voices could be heard in conversation, for the greater part in an unintelligible undertone, but at intervals rising so that they could be plainly overheard.

"Dost make out who it is that is speaking"? the astrologer asked in a whisper.

"One voice rises familiarly on my ears," returned the secretary.

"Hush"! enjoined the astrologer. "It is that of thine enemy, Prasad Singh. Wait patiently and listen."

Bipin shivered. A groan of terror was only suppressed by the greater fear of being discovered.

Presently the voice unknown to Bipin asked a question, distinctly heard without.

"Dost think, my Lord, that sixty men will suffice for the affair"?

"They will be enough," returned that of the other speaker, which Bipin believed to come from the mouth of Prasad. "We will carry the palace by assault, and make away with everyone who intercepts our progress, until we reach the person of the Rani."

"To-morrow night thou hast determined on the attempt"?

"To-morrow night. Be careful to come to the place of meeting at the tomb of Firoz Khan near the lake, one hour before midnight."

"As thou commandest. Hast thou a particular desire to make a prisoner of anyone"?

"Aye truly have I," came the quick rejoinder. "Thou wilt secure but deal gently with that arch rascal, Bipin Dat."

Without, the astrologer clapped a hand over the secretary's mouth to prevent a wail of despair going forth upon the night.

"Set thy knees and teeth, worthy Secretary," whispered the astrologer, "or they will shake the heavens down upon our heads."

"Be very careful of him," continued the voice within, "as I have somewhat to say regarding his impertinence and presumption before cutting his nose and ears off, and flinging his liver to the dogs. Of all those about the Rani, him I detest the most."

Bipin sank an invertebrate bundle of humanity to the ground. He entwined his arms about the astrologer's legs in a mute appeal for protection. His throat was incapable of uttering a sound.

The astrologer stooped down and shook Bipin by the shoulder.

"Go," he urged in an imperative whisper, "if thou wouldst save thy life and that of others. Come, get upon thy feet. Fly to the Rani's presence, and disclose to her this accursed plot. Remember that the meeting place is the tomb of Firoz Khan at one hour before midnight, to-morrow. I would come with thee but my bones are old, and must remain to screen thy flight."

Bipin crawled on his hands and knees to a little distance, and then rising, ran as fast as his corpulency would permit, back in the direction of the city.

Of that journey he retained afterwards little recollection. More than once he fell over some obstacle in his path, to rise with bruised limbs and resume his terror-hounded course. He lost his slippers in a ditch, and his turban in a thicket, into which he had strayed in the darkness. Whether he entered the city by a gate or scaled the walls he knew not, but panting, scratched, and with disordered garments, the worthy secretary did at last reach the palace, and struggle in by the astonished servants.

At the hour of Bipin's return, the Rani was entertaining her court with a *natch* in one of the gardens. Among others, Ahmad Khan had availed himself of an invitation to be present, leaving his guest, Prasad, in a better humor than he had displayed for some days past. As a sign of reviving spirit, he had even promised the Mohammedan to take part in a boar hunt on the following morning. He had scarcely mentioned the Rani's name since the astrologer's visit of the day before, except to remark that he believed Mohurran Goshi's pills and charms were assisting him to control his passion.

By the light of torches the girls had delighted their audience with several exhibitions of their art. In an interval refreshments of sweetmeats and sherbet were being served, when the strange figure made by Bipin Dat broke through the half circle formed by the girls and musicians. Out of breath, with his dress in the utmost disorder, he waddled to the Rani's position, and with a groan sank down at her feet.

"Why, what is the meaning of this"? asked the Rani in accents of surprise. "Truly, O Bipin, thou must have been chased by the terrible white fox of which thou livest in such dread."

"O great Lady," moaned Bipin, casting his hands upward despairingly. "Alas! we are all, every one of us, now dead."

"Dead"! exclaimed the Rani. "Not quite dead yet, I think, good Secretary."

"Ah, hae, hae"! Bipin continued to moan piteously. "Dead, all dead," he groaned; "or before another moon has set, most assuredly we all will be."

"Now what dost thou mean by this nonsense"? demanded the Rani impatiently. "Speak, what has reduced thee to such a condition of distress. Thou art interrupting the pleasure of my guests."

A groan as if drawn from the pit of his stomach came forth from Bipin's lips.

"O Rani," he spoke hoarsely. "The accursed Prasad

Singh, may God send his soul into the body of a scorpion for ten thousand years, he—he——"

At the mention of the Hindu noble's name, the Rani started and gazed inquiringly upon Bipin, who hesitated, as if he knew not how to commence his horrifying disclosure.

"Well," urged the Rani. "Well, what of the noble Prasad Singh. What knowest thou of him"?

"Oh! great Rani. He—the accursed Prasad Singh plotteth——"

"Stay," interposed the Rani quickly. Stay Bipin, I will hear what thou hast to impart privately."

"Ahmad Khan," she said, turning to the Mohammedan. "As Prasad is thy guest, thou wilt come with us apart. Let the *natch* continue," she added to an attendant. "We will return presently."

She led the way to a corridor at one end of the garden and then addressed Bipin.

"Speak now what thou knowest of the noble Prasad Singh, and be certain that it is no idle tale, no unfounded gossip, or rest assured thou wilt suffer real pain without any doubt."

"Great Rani," returned Bipin plaintively. "Let my mouth be filled with dust, and my face shaved only on one side as an object of ridicule for all liars, if I do not speak the truth. From a wise man, for sometime have I been warned that Prasad Singh had evil designs upon my nose and ears. That——"

The Rani interposed with angry impatience.

"Thy nose and ears, fool! What would the noble Prasad Singh care for anything that pertaineth to thy life or person. Did I not warn thee not to trespass upon my good nature with such nonsense"?

Bipin assumed an expression of wounded dignity, but replied with submission.

"Noble Rani, that is as may be; but the same wise man to make plain to me Prasad Singh's accursed designs led me this evening to a meeting place, where, in seclusion, I heard Prasad discuss a plot to assault the palace to-morrow night. With six hundred, nay I believe it was six thousand followers, he will put everyone to the sword, seize your Highness's throne for himself, and, O great Lady, consign you for evermore to a fortress guarded by terrible monsters. And as for me, O noble one, alas"! Bipin whined in terror. "In revenge for my fidelity to thee, my nose and ears are to be cut off and nailed to the palace gate, and my body," he groaned deeply, "O holy Kali, chopped in pieces and cast to swine. Alas! what a miserable fate lieth in store for all of us."

The Rani was about to reply when Ahmad interposed angrily.

"What is all this thou sayest of the noble Prasad Singh? Dost know that thou art accusing a high and loyal prince of the vilest treachery. By the Prophet's beard! were it not that I regard thee as but a half witted fool, for such lies upon a friend, I would cut thee on the spot into the pieces of which thou speakest."

He made an impulsive motion with his hand toward the hilt of his sword, but the Rani restrained him.

"Stay Ahmad," she enjoined. "Perchance somewhere in all this mass of exaggeration there may lie a speck of truth. You must admit Prasad's actions of late might warrant a measure of suspicion."

"Noble Rani," replied Ahmad in a tone of excuse. "That Prasad Singh may have been guilty of youthful folly, that he has not paid due respect to your exalted office and person, I will not deny; but that he should harbor a single thought, far less attempt an act against your authority, I will swear it to be a lie upon the sacred book. Nay, more, I will defend his honor in such a matter, with my sword, against whoever may make the vile assertion."

"Ahmad," returned the Rani thoughtfully. "It is to thy credit that thou dost behold Prasad only with the eye of a friend; but I possess my own reason for searching further into this matter. Now Bipin," she continued addressing the secretary impressively, "state plainly, and without resort to a riot of thy nervous fancy, what thou hast actually seen and heard. As thou tellest the truth thou wilt meet with recompense, but if thou liest, I swear I will carry out the doom thou believest is in store for thee."

With numerous checks upon his tendency to wander from the main thread of his story, Bipin disclosed by degrees a full account of what he had overheard at the window of the hut outside the city. In spite of a strict cross examination on the part of the Rani and Ahmad Khan, he held steadfastly to two points, that it was Prasad's voice he had undoubtedly heard in the treasonable discussion, and that in his terrified condition he had entirely forgotten the name of the wise man who had conducted him to the spot.

Bipin's interrogation was brought finally to a conclusion. The Rani dismissed him with the assurance that he had acted wisely in her interest, and might fear no evil from any direction.

"Well, my Lord," she asked of Ahmad. "What do you now think of this"?

"Truly, noble Lady," he replied, "my understanding is still unable to give credence to such a report. I cannot believe it of my friend Prasad, staying as he is under the shelter of my roof. By not a sign or word has he intimated any such design to me. I thought him far too much consumed with the fair Ganga's charms to care for any project upon earth. Alas! one knows not what to think. So noble a fellow to fall into such evil paths."

The Rani bit her lip and clenched her hands tightly to restrain the burst of jealous passion called to the surface of her nature by the Mohammedan's insidious thrust.

"Noble Rani," petitioned Ahmad, "I beg thou wilt permit me to return immediately to my house. There, I will cautiously sound the noble Prasad on this matter, and if I find a grain of truth in the report, so display to him the ingratitude, the wickedness of such thoughts, that surely will he express his sorrow and hasten to thy presence abjectly craving pardon."

"Ah"! cried the Rani with bitter resentment in her voice. "If it be true, think not that I will accept his repentance or grant a pardon. Nay Ahmad, thou art not to breathe a word of this to any mortal being, or thou shalt fall under my unchangeable displeasure. For the moment it is my intention to be present at this meeting in the tomb of Firoz Khan, and if he be found plotting this damnable deceit, may the Gods of India help him, for the Rani will show no mercy."

The darkness concealed a smile of supreme triumph on the Mohammedan's face.

"As thou commandest, noble one," he replied in a voice of regretful emotion. "I pray to *Allah* that it may be proved this fool's wits have gone far wandering than that my friend doth contemplate such inconceivable treachery. How doth the noble Rani purpose to act further"? he asked.

"That, Ahmad, I am considering," she replied.

She continued in a part soliloquy:

"If Prasad is bent upon this mischief, there is no doubt he will gather to his side a following. Divide Bipin's last total in half, and there would yet remain thirty unhanged rascals. Why should not I number myself as one of them"?

"But consider the danger, noble Lady," protested Ahmad. He was astonished at the daring of the Rani's project.

"What care I for danger"? she returned in an off-hand manner. "Surely you, above all men, will not deny that in the peril of a desperate situation, there lies more charm than can be gained from watching yonder seductive *natch*."

"Aye for a man of arms, fair Lady. But thou art a woman."

"And a Maratha born," she answered significantly. "Forget not that, O Ahmad. Not even yet dost thou know the Rani of Jhansi. By God's favor I will some day, perhaps, fight sword in hand on horseback with the bravest of you."

The dauntless spirit of her nature appealed to a counterpart in the Mohammedan's character in a way that no other human quality could have done. Though he realized it not, it was this force of her being that held him bound to her service, in a sense, a comrade, as much as he was a lover.

He murmured a genuine tribute of his admiration.

"Truly, I will not say thee nay, brave Rani. But how then wouldst thou proceed. Surely thou wilt not go alone into this affair"?

"No," she resumed. "I do not intend Prasad to gain quite so much advantage. One against thirty would be too unequal odds to combat. With me, Rati, shall number another of these villains, and within the summons of my voice, thou wilt hold my Valaiti bodyguard in some convenient place of hiding. Such can be done, can it not, good Ahmad"?

"I know just such a place close to the tomb," he replied.

"Then it is well or ill," she replied, "whichever way we may regard it. To-morrow I, too, will keep an unexpected tryst with Prasad at the tomb of Firoz Khan, and if he be there, as it hath been reported, the Rani will herself determine how to deal with him. Come! let us return now to the *natch*. Let no one suspect that anything hath gone amiss."

Ahmad paused with a gesture of appeal.

"May I not, O just Rani, say but one word for him who is my friend"?

"Nay, not one," she answered. "If he be found innocent he hath committed no offense against the Rani; if guilty, he hath well merited his punishment. Come"! she urged impatiently.

With dejected mien, Ahmad obediently followed.

When the *natch* was over, he strode hurriedly from the palace. He made his way quickly to Mohurran Goshi's home, and called the astrologer from his slumbers.

"But a word with thee, learned Doctor," he whispered at the door. "Our star could not shine brighter. All goes well; but the Rani and one of her women are to make two of Prasad's following. Dost understand"?

The astrologer intimated that he would look to the addition of two to the original number, provided for the Hindu noble's purpose."

"Then good fortune to us all," concluded Ahmad. "The shadow of the accursed Prasad vanishes as beneath the sun at noonday."

Chapter XIV

AT THE TOMB OF FIROZ KHAN

THE city of the Rani slept. The bazaars and side streets were deserted. But for an occasional light gleaming fitfully through a half opened casement, and the dark forms of sentinels pacing back and forth in noiseless tread upon the walls, Jhansi might have been a city of the dead. In countless, glittering myriads, the heavenly bodies strode majestically in their eternal courses above the silent night. By the mercy of the supreme Parem-eswara, the labor of the day completed with the departing sun, the people had lain down to rest; their joys, sorrows, hopes, for a space, gathered into oblivion. Thus Jhansi slept.

Three figures habited in male attire approached the eastern gate, and gave a password. The gate was slowly opened, and the three went forth. Behind them, the massive portals swung back into place upon grating hinges.

Direct from the lofty, frowning bastion, a road led toward the summer palace on the borders of the lake. Here and there clumps of tamarind and acacia rose indistinctly on either side of the way. Rapidly, yet with caution to avoid intercepting the nocturnal adventure of some poisonous reptile, the three directed their steps along the road. Their feet impressed the thick coating of dust noiselessly. Not a word was exchanged, and no sound broke upon their ears save the occasional yelping of a startled cur or the dismal cry of a jackal summoning a companion to a scent of prey. Once, only, a solitary figure met them at a little distance from the city. If bent upon evil, he concealed his purpose by a greeting of peace.

"The blessing of God be with you," he cried.

"And with you, O Stranger, peace," the foremost of the three answered in a woman's voice, despite the conflicting evidence of her dress.

Presently they came to a parting of the road. A narrow path led amid a growth of trees to the brink of the lake. Massively the white square walls of the tomb of Firoz Khan, with its central dome became visible through the branches. The party halted.

"What now, my Lord"? the owner of the voice that had returned the wayfarer's salutation asked.

"Noble Rani," that of Ahmad Khan replied, "yonder is our destination. Behind the wall thou canst just discern to the right, lie, well concealed, a hundred of thy Valaiti bodyguard; but I know not if the conspirators are assembled."

At the moment a white cloth was waved thrice above the wall. Ahmad evidently took it for a signal. He spoke in a low tone.

"Whoever the villains may be, they are now gathered together. Here I will leave thee to pass in hiding to the guard, while if thou art still determined upon the enterprise, thou hadst better advance boldly to the entrance. For the rest, I make no doubt thine own judgment and discretion, will serve thee better than any advice of mine."

"Well said, my faithful Ahmad," the Rani answered. "Thou art certain to hear my call if need be from yonder hiding place"?

"Were it softer than the note of the bulbul, fair Lady, be assured, it would reach me even at the gate of Paradise."

Thus while Ahmad stealthily disappeared among the trees, the Rani motioned her waiting woman to follow, and proceeded fearlessly toward the entrance of the tomb.

That those within had taken measures to prevent a surprise was demonstrated by a challenge the moment that the Rani emerged into the open space about the building.

"Stand! who comes"? a voice demanded.

The Rani replied promptly in firm accents. "Two followers of the noble Prasad Singh."

A short period of consultation among the conspirators apparently ensued. Without, the Rani awaited the answer with deep emotion. Would the report prove true or false, that he whom she loved was a traitor as well as a libertine?

Presently the response came.

"It is well, advance."

"Alas! it is ill," her heart murmured. "Ah God! the ingratitude, the cruelty of it."

She advanced to the open door and entered the main chamber of the tomb. A shaded lamp dimly illuminated the interior. Her glance swept quickly from the five or six armed men gathered in a group, to a stalwart form she intuitively recognized as that of Prasad Singh, in spite of the disguise he had assumed. He was pacing to and fro a little apart from his companions, as if impatient of some detail of his plan yet to be completed.

He turned quickly on her entrance and spoke in a voice of stern rebuke.

"Thou art late," he exclaimed. "Thou hast kept us waiting long after the appointed hour."

"Pardon, my Lord," replied the Rani, halting in the dark shadow of a pillar. "Our steps were misdirected."

"A curse upon the muddled brain of that astrologer," he muttered. "Now hearken, while I tell thee briefly, what I have impressed upon thy comrades at some length. We go now to the city as belated travelers, with an admission at the gate that hath already been assured. Thou wilt then follow my steps quickly and silently to the Rani's palace. As the others have their allotted duty, thou wilt seek the garden gate and hold it securely so that no one passes in or forth. If force be threatened thou wilt in like manner threaten force, aye, and use it if so need be. Thou hast arms"? he asked.

"Aye, noble captain," she replied. "Arms have we. But if the Rani doth herself come forth. What then, great sir"? she questioned in return.

"Thou wilt detain her above all others, though careful to do her no personal harm," he enjoined emphatically.

"But should she command us to let her pass, my

Lord"? she pressed still further, in a quiet, assumed voice.

"Thou wilt obey the command of him who payeth thee for thy service, thou idle questioner," he returned. "Thy order is to hold her securely until my pleasure concerning her hath been learned."

There followed a momentary pause, then her voice rose solemnly to the vaulted roof.

"My Lord Raja, Prasad Singh, thou hast no need to go to Jhansi for the Rani. Behold she is now before thee."

She moved from the shadow and stood confronting him, an expression of offended dignity visible upon her face.

He uttered an exclamation of surprise mingled with dismay. Impulsively he strode forward.

"Stand where thou art," she commanded. "Move not a pace, a man of you, for at the raising of my voice a hundred troopers, lying at hand, will hasten to my side."

With a muttered oath Prasad halted, while the Rani turned to the door and summoned Ahmad.

Almost upon the instant the Mohammedan noble and a score of the Rani's bodyguard appeared before the entrance.

"Alas, Ahmad," she said. "Our hope is dashed in pieces as a pitcher hurled upon a rock. Bipin, poor fellow, hath earned my displeasure as well as my gratitude for the truth that he has told. I would now, that I could recompense him for being a liar concerning this night's work. Take these duped fools into safe keeping, and then await my order. I will speak with Prasad first."

She motioned the shrinking forms inside the chamber to pass without, and remained alone with Prasad.

For several minutes there reigned an unbroken silence, as the Rani and her guilty lover stood face to face. The moon had risen over the lake and sent its pale light through a crevice in the dome of the ruined tomb. It marked by deep shadows the recesses, and filled the chamber with an atmosphere in sympathy with the chill that seized upon the heart of the woman.

She spoke at last in a measured tone.

"How, now, my Lord Prasad Singh. A short while since you said the Rani was to be held until she heard your pleasure. Behold, she now patiently awaiteth it. What wilt thou do with her"?

Prasad hesitated a moment, then cast himself at her feet.

"Taunt me not, noble one," he petitioned. "I do not seek thy pardon; but I do ask thee to hear me speak."

"Aye, will I," came the response coldly. "Is it not to hear what thou canst say for such surprising conduct that I am now waiting on thy words."

"As God sees my heart, my sole excuse is my all consuming love for thee."

"Thy love for me," she echoed. "Surely it is a most unusual way of showing it, good Prasad. Thou gatherest here a company of rascals to assault my palace, and order them to heed not my command, to hold me a prisoner until I shall learn thy pleasure. Thy love for me. Oh "! she cried with a note of scorn in her voice. " Thou must indeed cherish a constant love for me."

" Ah, fair one, be not so ungracious," he besought her. " Surely thou hast tried me more than I was able to endure."

" I tried thee," she repeated bitterly. " Aye, I did try thee, and thou hast proved to be most woefully amiss. What art thou, a drinker of spirits, a libertine, and Ah God! a traitor to thy Queen."

Stung by her accusations he sprang passionately to his feet.

" It is not true," he retorted hotly. " Upon all things sacred do I swear to it."

" Aye, thou art in a fitting situation for thy oath to carry weight," she answered; " but, believe me I care not for thy escapades with *natch* girls, or thy drunken orgies. Of such I do not look for an account. Thy reason for this company is what I seek."

" Some accursed villain hath betrayed me," he muttered fiercely. " That dog of an astrologer, or can it be my good Moslem friend, the noble Ahmad Khan "?

" Nay," she replied sorrowfully. " It is thine own false heart, O Prasad, that hath betrayed thee. I know of no astrologer, and as for Ahmad Khan, thou art only adding an injustice to thy other wickedness by slandering the fidelity of a friend. Even when this villainy of thine was made plain to me, he it was who stood firm as a champion of thy miserable faith. I doubt not that now his heart is sore with grief."

"Then fair Lady," he exclaimed. "Since the Gods have willed it, that I shall appear in thine eyes as the vilest of creatures, life hath no more object. Take it, O Rani. I yield it to thee as readily here, as I would have done for thee amid the press of battle."

He drew a dagger from his girdle and offered the handle to the Rani. He bowed his head submissively.

She gazed upon him with sorrowful eyes. She took the dagger from him and for a moment grasped it tightly. Would she plunge it to his heart? He waited resignedly. It would be an act of mercy was his only thought.

Then she spoke in slow accents, first sternly, but toward the close with a quaver in her voice.

"As the Rani, I could, O Prasad, kill thee; but as Lachmi Bai thou—thou art forgiven. Oh! why hast thou thus treated me"?

The dagger flashed with a clatter to the pavement; her hand dropped listlessly to her side.

With a sudden burst of joy in his heart and arms outstretched, he stepped forward, prompted by an impulse of the moment.

She waved him back imperiously.

"Nay, I command, do thou not touch me. If thou art forgiven by Lachmi Bai, thou art not pardoned by the Jhansi Rani. Thy life she hath returned to thee that thou mayest redeem thine honor by honorable deeds, but thou canst not remain in Jhansi."

He drew back with dejection stamped upon his face.

She turned to the door and summoned Ahmad Khan.

The Mohammedan responded with reluctant steps. He paused on beholding Prasad, sighed deeply, and directed his eyes toward the ground.

"Ahmad," she commanded. "It is my wish that thou dost now conduct the noble Prasad Singh safely to the boundary of the state. He doth leave me with a message to the Rao Sahib."

She added this from the desire to screen the Hindu noble's public downfall.

"Noble Lady," petitioned Ahmad, ignoring her intention. "Thou placest on my shoulders too heavy a burden. Prasad Singh hath grown to be my friend. I cannot regard or hold one as a prisoner who hath so recently been my honored guest. I beg thou wilt depute this unhappy duty to another, such as thy faithful servant, the Dost Ali Khan, now without."

"By Heaven"! cried Prasad angrily, a wave of jealousy sweeping all other feeling to the winds. "To such indignity I will not submit."

He stooped and seizing the dagger that had remained upon the floor, stood at bay defiantly.

For a moment surprise was depicted on the Rani's face, then she sought his reason.

"Why dost thou so object to the escort of Dost Ali"? she asked innocently.

"Thou askest me why I should object to this Dost Ali"? he retorted. "No," he laughed mockingly. "In pleasant company forsooth with thy——"

Something in the Rani's expression appealed direct to his sense of honor, checking him in the utterance of the final word. Fortunately it died upon his lips unspoken.

As if she had penetrated his meaning the Rani started, her countenance menacing with sudden passion. She clutched Ahmad so tightly by the wrist that he was forced to set his teeth to withhold an oath of pain.

The situation was also critical for him. If the Rani were to accept the implied challenge of her virtue, the result might be a disclosure of his deep intrigue.

The danger, for Ahmad, passed as she replied with an effort of controlled emotion.

"Truly thou art mad, O Prasad. Thy folly and passion doth almost accomplish its inevitable end. Fortunate is it, those who wish thee well have pity for thee. To reason with thee would only be an act, equally insane."

She walked toward him fearlessly and laid her hand upon the dagger hilt.

"Come," she enjoined. "Thou hast surrendered. Thou shalt obey my will within my state, even if it be my pleasure that Dost Ali doth accompany thee to the boundary."

"A curse upon thy pleasure," retorted Prasad sullenly, relinquishing the dagger to her hand. The sooner that my feet are free from this unlucky soil, perchance the more quickly will I gain some peace of mind. I care not how I leave it, so I ride forth speedily."

"Ah! in truth, good Prasad, how well dost thou display thy penitence," she answered reproachfully. "This dagger will I hold as a pledge for thy better nature yet to claim. Farewell, my Lord. I pray a kindlier fortune may attend our next meeting."

She moved toward the door, and pausing, turned upon him a look of deep regret.

Prasad's countenance betrayed no change of feeling.

The Rani passed out into the moonlight, where her troopers had grouped themselves about the tomb. Ahmad followed. He begged to know her wish concerning the other prisoners.

"Carry them also to the boundary," she ordered, "and let them go to whatever place God wills. I pray I may never set eyes on one of them again."

"Doth the Rani now wish to return to Jhansi"? he asked, "or will she accept the poor hospitality of Ahmad Khan. His house is within a little distance."

"Not now, good Ahmad," she replied. "I would be for a short time alone. Remain here with those unneeded for the escort, while I go yonder to the shrine. Presently I will return."

She acknowledged the salute of the officers as they gazed with wonder on her masculine attire, and moved slowly amid the trees to the temple of the great god of Hindustan.

"Thanks be to Allah," Ahmad murmured devoutly. "This night is mine."

Black was the heart of the Mohammedan. The night was his—a night of hell riot loosened in his soul. Passion and murder struggled for the first place in his intention. Blood was already on his hands. Like a tiger his thirst for more was now unquenchable.

Mohurran Goshi called to his door earlier in the evening had received his unreckoned due. Ahmad's dagger had forever settled the account between them. The wise discerner of other's good and evil fortune, had failed to calculate his own swiftly approaching end.

In like manner a secret order to Dost Ali was to terminate the conspirators' existence. Ahmad quickly planned that in some dark ravine, before the boundary was reached, the deed might be easily accomplished. Prasad to be dispatched in revenge, the others as a safer fetter than money upon their silence. He quickly selected the escort, and then drew Dost Ali to one side.

"It is the Rani's command, O discreet Ali," he said in an undertone, "that these rascals are to be conducted to the boundary; but thou wilt easily gather her implied meaning. She declared she doth hope never to set eyes on any one of them again. Dost understand, she trusteth to thy sword, that not one of them may by chance return."

Dost Ali drew himself up and replied tersely.

"I understand her command that they are to be set free at the boundary."

"By Allah"! exclaimed Ahmad petulantly. "Thy mind doth evidence little penetration. "Clearly she doth not wish them to be set free at the boundary, but in some convenient spot dispatched from further harm."

"If such be her meaning," replied the other firmly, "she must express it thus to me in words. Too well do I know my duty to place an interpretation of my own upon her plain command. As the order stands, I will escort them to the boundary."

An exclamation of impatience burst from Ahmad's lips. The moment was opportune for a still more wicked design. It left him no time to argue the matter further.

"Then get thee gone upon thy business," he retorted angrily. "For all my trouble I see thou art poorly witted to rise in favor at the Rani's court. Thy stupidity will interpose between a great reward."

"To obey an order strictly was ever the injunction of my illustrious teacher, Dost Mohammed Khan," the young officer replied firmly. "Alone, by so doing, do I seek reward."

He saluted Ahmad haughtily, and turned to order the mounting of his command.

"A curse upon the fool," muttered Ahmad fiercely. "Who could have reckoned on a conscience from the Afghan school? But that the hour has come to gratify a yearning hunger, I would beat submission to his brain."

He bade the rest of the troopers await his return, and set forth in the opposite direction taken by the Rani. When beyond the range of observation from the tomb, he turned, and quickly but cautiously made a *detour* with the temple also, as his destination.

In his mind he beheld the woman of his passionate desire, practically alone and unprotected. To the priests and attendants he wasted not a thought. They would fly in terror at the first cry of alarm. She, for whom he had jeopardized his soul by swearing falsely on the Koran would then remain to suffer willingly or otherwise the purpose of his mind. That the ground was sacred, mattered not. Dedicated to a heathen God, it would have been an act of his faith to slaughter the priests and raze the building to the ground. More, was not she, also, an unbeliever, given into his embrace by the will of God. When accomplished, a swift horse in waiting, would, if need be, carry him far distant from the vengeance of the outraged woman. Of that he had not been unmindful.

The Rani had approached the temple with sorrow consuming her heart. Her affection for Prasad had gone forth spontaneously almost at their first meeting. She had beheld in him what she believed to be her ideal of a chivalrous noble. That he possessed failings due to youth and inexperience she was ready to admit; but that he should prove such a hopeless failure in all his qualities, was a bitter disappointment. A drunkard, a consort of other women, while he asserted his unalterable love for her, a conspirator against her authority if not her person, surely her affection could not have been bestowed upon a more worthless object. Her temperament was not such as to display her anguish by lamenting Prasad's faithlessness and her own wrong into every willing ear; but none the less was there the necessity to obtain relief by an, outpouring of her spirit. In secret, before the great God she worshipped, she purposed to seek consolation for her wounded heart; then to go forth and bear outwardly before her people no trace of her inward grief.

The temple was wrapt in silence. In the outer building white robed, recumbent figures of priests and attendants lay here and there where they had chosen a resting place. With hushed steps the Rani stole past these, crossed a courtyard, and entered the chamber of the God. Save for the glow from an incense burner, the interior was veiled in darkness, to emphasize the unknown mysterious element of Siva's being. Before her, the figure of the God loomed a darker object, seated upon an altar pedestal, wrapt in profound, eternal meditation. The morrow was a festival and flowers had already been bountifully scattered upon the altar, and, in wreaths, hung about the person of the sacred image. She stood for a moment before the shrine, then knelt in prayer.

" O great Siva," she petitioned. " All wise, all powerful, all just God, Protector of Animals, Vanquisher of Death; thou, whose vision and understanding doth penetrate all things from the infinitude of Heaven to the deepest secrets of the human soul, behold the unhappiness of thy daughter. Striving to be just yet ever suffering injustice, to appease jealousy but to behold new dissension rise on every hand, and O Holy God, loving only to receive ingratitude and faithlessness in return. Give me, I beg of thee, above all things, a spirit of resolute courage to combat the vicissitudes of life, and to hold death powerless of terror in whatever form it shall come. Aye, and O Great God, give to me this divine quality so that I may inspire the faltering hearts of others, if need be to valiant deeds for the honor of our faith and country."

She raised her face upward to the protecting hands of the God, and remained thus in silent communion.

Ahmad Khan, too, approached the temple, and passed by the sleeping figures. With noiseless tread he crossed the court, and stood upon the threshold of the shrine. Before him, the woman still knelt in wrapt devotion. For a moment his eyes feasted on her captivating form. Ah *Allah!* his at last.

With the prize seeming to his hand, the intoxication of the moment stayed his grasp. His opportunity was lost. A cry near by, shrill and prolonged, as of a beast relentlessly attacked by some more powerful adversary, rose upon the night. It echoed within the temple. The Rani started to her feet as Ahmad took a hasty stride forward. She seized a torch at hand and thrust it into the incense burner. Then facing him, she held it high above her head.

Ahmad halted suddenly and trembled.

The figure of the Rani, majestic and awe inspiring, posed before the dark image of the God, thrilled his soul with a first sensation of terror. She appeared to gaze full upon him, yet beheld him not. Her stature seemed to rise visibly before his eyes. The light of the torch flaring upward cast into strong relief the ornate decorations of the shrine, the countenance of Siva no longer buried in thought; but, in his non-Aryan aspect, wrathful and menacing. Her lips moved, but no sound came forth. She appeared to be enveloped in an ecstatic dream.

Before his fixed gaze, strange beings floated in the air. Ancient Vedic Gods, the bright and shining ones. Indra the rain bringer, Agni the God of fire, Vayu of the wind, Rudra the ruler of the tempest; their very names long since buried in oblivion to the multitude.

They gathered about the transfigured form of the Rani, as if to protect her from a shadow of harm.

Was the scene but the effect of a feverish imagination? In contradiction to the tenets of his religion, superstitious of all that was visionary and inexplicable, Ahmad was ready to believe the whole a dread reality, a manifestation of divine blessing resting upon the head of the girl.

He would have cried aloud for mercy, but terror had bereft his tongue of speech. He clasped his brow tightly. For a moment he reeled, then fell to the pavement.

The night was lost and won.

Chapter XV

IN THE COURSE OF EVENTS

MANY days had passed beneath the Rani's feet. Almost hourly the loom of peril rose threateningly upon her position. From every source, with unrelenting persistence, the worst news came to shatter the hopes of those who had espoused the Native cause in Jhansi.

First the report of the recapture and looting of Delhi was confirmed; to which was added the intelligence that the aged Emperor was a prisoner in the enemy's hands, and that his sons had been slaughtered. Then that Lucknow was relieved, and the army of the Peshwa put to flight. Reports of other reverses succeeded one another with disheartening rapidity.

The hour of the Foreigners' vengeance had come. Terror was the weapon they now wielded to crush the rebellion. It was not without satisfactory result in the interest of their dominion in India. The undisciplined mobs led by generals suspicious of each other's actions melted away before the impetuous onslaughts of the white men. Many Native leaders sought to make peace while the hour of grace lasted. Those still wavering quickly made up their minds that they had ever loved the Foreigner as a parent.

But for those taken in open revolt it was soon made plain that there was to be no mercy. They were blown from the mouths of cannon to end their lives in this world, and, according to the belief of the sentenced, to exterminate their existence in the next. The demand rose that as a lasting memorial of the triumph of the Christian faith as well as of the Christian sword over both Hindu and Mohammedan, temples should be converted into churches, and that on every tile of the Great Mosque at Delhi a martyr's name should be engraved.

In another part of the world the names of Christian martyrs may be seen cut into the walls of subterranean passages bearing witness to a triumph of their faith brought about by other means. But it was the Nineteenth and not the Third Century. It was Cawnpur and not the Coliseum to be avenged.

Reports of these things, also, came to the Rani's ears. "See," she cried, "how faithfully do these Foreigners observe the commandments of their gentle Prophet. Were a Mohammedan conqueror raging through the land, his injunction to plunder and spare none could not be more swiftly obeyed."

With the news of each fresh disaster, the number of dismayed faces turned toward the Rani increased proportionately; but upon her countenance there was no reflection of the weakening sentiment. Her spirit rose as that of an eagle threatened with the destruction of its young. She realized that time was bringing for her, a supreme test of forethought and endurance, as well as of courage.

As she had surprised all with the wisdom displayed

in the conduct of her civil government—a curious reproach to those who had regarded her as incapable to occupy a throne—her military judgment was marked by intuitive sagacity of the highest merit.

On the ramparts of the rock fortress new guns were mounted commanding the whole plain; the massive walls surrounding the city on its three other sides were repaired; the mamelon, or mound, at the south-east corner, together with several flanking bastions, armed, so that they bristled with guns. With untiring perseverance she had collected and trained to a state of efficiency a defending force of eleven thousand men, every one of whom had sworn to defend her person and honor to the last extremity.

Thus her outward life displayed no sign of the unhealed wound in her heart. Of Prasad, she had received no intelligence directly. Rumor had upon occasion reported his presence with the standard of the Native general, Tantia Topi, so far victorious and vanquished in turn. Ahmad Khan still remained as the most obedient of her lieutenants.

From the pavement of the temple he had risen to go forth with a new feeling regarding her. The element of his passion still remained, but the absence of his rival cast the stimulant of jealousy into abeyance, and a belief that in some way her person was sacred, prevented any present contemplation of a renewal of his suit to the point of overt action. Once only had he ventured with humility to touch upon his unrequited sentiment. She quickly divined the purpose of his mind, and interposed before a declaration.

"Greatly do I appreciate thy faithful service, O Ahmad," she said, "and in the strife I fear is quickly approaching, there is no one of whose aid I would less willingly be deprived; but of thy longing for my deeper affection thou must not speak again. Long since have I given my love to the welfare of my people, to naught else."

A sigh lightly escaped her lips. For a moment her gaze passed from the immediate scene. Perhaps it sought the figure of a young noble fighting bravely on some far off battlefield.

"Fair Lady," Ahmad petitioned. "Canst thou not give me but a grain of hope"?

"Hope, Ahmad," she replied evasively, "of one kind and another we may each cherish. It is well, for we know not what lies before us on the morrow. Alas! we are as butterflies dancing in the sunlight. A cloud sweeps across the Heavens, and behold, we and our hopes have vanished."

With the worthy secretary, Bipin Dat, unhappy even in the happiness of the banishment of his fancied enemy, and relief from the terrors held over him by his late counselor, Mohurran Goshi; he was not slow to discover another astrologer, who was quite ready to lighten the weight of a well filled purse, in exchange for prognostications of extraordinary good fortune. But the secretary's horoscope was, it seemed, ever temporarily clouded by ominous signs, that could be dispelled for a consideration. As with others of the populace, a real terror rose above the horizon in the threatened return of the Foreigners. It served to recall to Bipin's mind the fact that a long period had elapsed since he had visited his family, dwelling in a province removed from the seat of war. It was a remarkable coincidence that with the daily advent of evil tidings, this filial sentiment grew stronger within him. By day it interfered with his digestion; at night it disturbed his rest. A final decision was brought about through the attempt of a creditor to recover an overdue account. Money that should have repaid the services of his barber, had been diverted into the rapacious purse of the new astrologer; and the barber was wrathful, even vindictive, in consequence. He took the usual course to enforce payment by an endeavor to shame the unworthy secretary in public.

Bipin sat in the shade of a pillar endeavoring to propitiate the barber with compliments, while a blunt razor was unmercifully scraped back and forth over his head. The mirror he held, in which to admire his features during the progress of his toilet, reflected a wry countenance.

"A handsome boy, that is of yours, most skilful Barber," he remarked; as the barber grasped his customer's nose in a tight pinch.

"Ah, yes," returned the barber dryly. "As thou sayest, I would like him to enter the Rani's service but that all her attendants will shortly be killed. *Ah, hae!* Alas!

The Foreigners now advancing will not let one of them escape."

He swept the razor significantly across Bipin's throat.

Bipin started.

"What is that you say"? he asked.

"Be careful, good sir," enjoined the barber, "or I might damage an ear destined for the Foreigners to cut off, after the city has been carried by assault."

Bipin shivered both in body and spirit. He mentally cursed the fate that seemed bent upon depriving him of his organs.

"Thou art a chicken hearted rogue of a barber," he replied excitedly, in an endeavor to overcome the shock to his courage. "Dost know that her Highness numbers among her followers some of the bravest fighters in the land, who will drive away the Foreigners as deer before tigers. Though not born to the sword, if such danger comes, I, myself, will bear arms and fight upon the walls."

The barber laughed tauntingly. His object was to incite the secretary's anger to the point of an open squabble, so that he could then proclaim his wrong and obtain payment through the adverse criticism that would fall on Bipin's head.

"You fight, worthy Secretary," he sneered. "Why a jackal would laugh at your valor. You would run at the first discharge of a gun, but that you are too fat, too corpulent."

Bipin struggled out of the barber's clutches, burning

with passion, half shaved, a delightful object of ridicule.

"Too fat," he gasped, striking the barber with the palm of his hand. "Too fat, thou lean ghost. If the accursed Foreigners catch thee, be assured thy bones will rattle well from the bough of a tree."

Instantly the hubbub the barber looked for rose. A dozen bystanders interfered, barking dogs rushed from corners, a score of voices clamored in the interest of they knew not what. Above it all, the wail of the barber proclaimed the secretary's remissness in his payment.

Bipin soon perceived the disadvantage of his situation. He was in the wrong, that was made plain. Reluctantly he drew forth the required sum and begged the offended barber take his money.

The offended barber at first swore by his God not to touch the smallest coin, but at last yielded to persuasion. He even accepted an additional payment as a solace for the personal affront, declared Bipin was to him as an uncle, and vowed that unless permitted to proceed with the shaving, the joy of his life would go out.

Thus peace was restored, the dogs slunk back to their corners, the bystanders directed their attention to other matters, and Bipin again gave his head to the hands of the now obsequious barber. But his mind was ill at ease.

"The razor shaves to your liking, I trust, great sir," remarked the barber, as he removed the roots as well as the stems of a tuft of Bipin's hair.

Bipin groaned with the pain, but from oft repeated similar experiences, continued to submit patiently.

"At least no worse than usual," he muttered in response. "But tell me what thou hast heard about the return of the Foreigners."

"Oh, little of any consequence," replied the barber light-heartedly. "They are on the road that will surely carry them off the face of the earth. The Rani's troops will rout them utterly. Thou wouldst make a fine soldier, worthy Secretary," he added in accents of admiration. "A brave figure on a horse."

"Perhaps so," returned Bipin dubiously. "What you say may be true, but at present I am considering another matter of importance. When is it reported in the bazaars that these Foreigners are likely to arrive"?

"Noble Secretary, that is not certain. Indeed, it is the general opinion they will never arrive except as prisoners."

The expression on Bipin's face did not reflect the barber's sudden optimism. In his mind he beheld the much more secure retreat afforded by the abode of his family while the road was still open. At the conclusion of his toilet he sought the Rani's presence.

A secret council of war had just been held. A messenger that morning had brought news of the rout of the Native army at Mandanpur only eighty miles distant from Jhansi, leaving the whole intervening country exposed, with the single exception of the fort of Chanderi.

There was no longer any doubt of the swift approach of the enemy, the only question being whether to give battle at some advantageous point, or defend the city until a relieving force could arrive under Tantia Topi. The question still awaited a final decision. The Rani herself was in favor of the former course, while her officers, with the exception of Ahmad Khan, strenuously urged the latter as more prudent. Another council was to meet later in the day upon the receipt of further expected intelligence.

Bipin *salaamed* and proceeded to introduce his request for leave of absence to visit his family, by a complimentary preface on the peaceful condition of all things under the shadow of the Rani's authority.

" Peace it may be for the moment, good Bipin," she interposed, in his word ramble over the whole State of Jhansi. " But assuredly to-morrow will find us all with arms in our hands."

Bipin affected astonishment. As he had been excluded from the council of war the news of the near approach of the Foreigners had not reached his ears. Was it possible that some audacious raja contemplated a revolt? he asked. Undoubtedly he would soon be brought to terms, and the Rani continue to reign undisturbed for evermore.

The Rani shook her head seriously.

" Thou wilt hear of it all quickly enough," she replied. " But in the meantime what is it thou desirest, for assuredly thou hast a petition "?

Bipin then launched forth into the disturbed state of his conscience on account of the long period which had elapsed since he had beheld his dear parents, his honored uncles, his worthy brothers, and all the host of his other relatives.

"Alas! noble Lady," he reflected contritely. "What will they think of their undutiful son. Most unfortunate would it be if they should consider that in the exalted state in which it has pleased your Highness to place me, I had forgotten their less fortunate condition. To explain that only the burden of my office has kept me from them, is the object of my seeking a few days absence from your Illustrious Greatness's side."

The Rani smiled in spite of the anxiety in her mind. "That is surely a most estimable desire, O Bipin," she replied. "But I would suggest that instead of taking so toilsome a journey, thou dost make thy regrets by letter, accompanied by a handsome present out of thy savings. In that way, be assured, they will be well satisfied."

Bipin's round face lengthened. The suggestion did not at all coincide with his present inclination.

"Noble Lady," he resumed gravely. "This would I gladly do, but that there are some family matters that can only be discussed with propriety by word of mouth."

"Then, good Bipin, thou must depart, I suppose," she replied, "though we shall be the loser by thy absence. But thou must use great caution on the journey," she added naively, "for the horsemen of the Foreigners may have already swept to the north, and if they catch thee, as a servant of the Jhansi Rani, I fear thou wilt never behold the faces of thy genial uncles."

An expression of indecision broke over Bipin's countenance. In that case, he quickly reasoned, the walls of Jhansi would undoubtedly be a safer retreat than the open highway.

"Then, perhaps, great Rani," he faltered, "I had better defer my visit for a season. Not for a mountain of gold would I be absent from thy side in the hour of danger. Upon my head would forever rest the reproach that I had turned my heels to the enemy."

"Nay," she answered thoughtfully. "Thou mayest go in safety, for as thy road lies by the camp of Tantia Topi, thou canst be of service by bearing a message to him from me. Thus far, an escort shall accompany thee. But thou must be ready to start immediately."

Bipin's face brightened visibly.

"I am ready even now, noble Lady," he replied, "and doubt not, will return with all speed in time to assist in the defeat of the Foreigners, should they venture to direct their steps toward Jhansi."

"Then take thy writing materials and set down as I dictate," she commanded.

Bipin produced a pen, a bottle of ink, and a pad; when the Rani delivered an urgent message to the Maratha general, setting forth the impending danger, and begging him to come speedily to her assistance.

Within an hour Bipin's whole attention was directed toward a heroic endeavor to keep his seat in the saddle of a spirited horse, while the troopers unsympathetically set a rapid pace along the road to Charkari.

Chapter XVI

JHANSI BESIEGED

HIGH above the city and the plain, from the loftiest pinnacle of the fortress, the banner of the Rani waved in proud defiance. The city gates were still open to admit a few stragglers fleeing to swell the overcrowded caravansaries. The incessant bleating of goats and sheep, mingled with the lowing of cattle, that rose above the human turmoil, proclaimed forethought in sweeping the country bare of all live stock, available as food for the advancing enemy. With similar prudence, the already arid coloring of the land had been hastened and intensified by the action of the Rani, in setting fire to the scrub jungle for miles in all directions. By this means the horses and baggage animals of the invading force would be deprived of local sustenance.

By the eastern gate a group of horsemen were held in momentary readiness to dash forth upon an urgent mission.

From a commanding point on the walls of the citadel, the Rani, Ahmad Khan, Dost Ali, and others of her officers, anxiously scanned the uneven horizon to the southward. Her arms rested on the parapet from which the rock fell away in a sheer precipice to the plain below. To the east of the city beyond the lake, the waters of the

Betwa, gleaming in the afternoon sunshine, wound a sinuous course northward. Directly beneath, the ruined bungalows of the Foreigners, the dismantled Star Fort near the cantonments, and temples amid shading clumps of tamarind, were indistinctly visible through the haze resting lightly upon the surface of the land.

The decision had been taken to defend the city instead of giving battle in the open. As a consequence the whole of the troops had been withdrawn from the cantonments to the walls. The latter presented an animated appearance, manned at all parts ready for the advent of the Foreigners.

The Rani gazing upon this scene, suddenly raised an arm and pointing afar off to a defile in the broken country, engaged Ahmad's attention.

"Look, my Lord," she cried. "Dost thou not make out some horsemen advancing yonder"?

Ahmad shaded his eyes with his hand, and for a few moments looked intently in the direction indicated.

"Aye," he replied at last. "They come on the Chanchanpur road. It must be the vanguard of the enemy."

He leaned over the parapet as if by a more earnest gaze to make sure of his opinion, then drew back with confirmation written on his face.

"Undoubtedly they are of the Foreign Sahib's army, my Lady Rani," he said. "I can tell by the action of their horses."

The Rani turned to a soldier standing to a gun near by. She raised her hand as a signal. Immediately a tongue of flame and a puff of white smoke shot forth from the muzzle of the cannon. The report that followed was borne above the city and echoed amid the crevices of the rock.

It had scarcely died away when similar reports boomed from rampart to bastion along the circuit of the walls, a prearranged warning of the Foreigners' approach. Commotion was manifested on the defenses as the soldiers hurried to their stations. Instantly the troop near the eastern gate clapped spurs to their horses' flanks and dashed forward on the road to Charkari. They bore a message to Tantia Topi, that Jhansi had been invested, and again called upon him for assistance. Behind them the gates swung back upon their hinges, drawbridges were raised, the siege of Jhansi had commenced.

The watchers on the citadel beheld the troop race for life along the Charkari road. They also beheld, with consternation, a flank movement by a detachment from the main body of the Foreign cavalry to intercept the messengers' escape.

"See, my Lord," the Rani cried anxiously, "the Foreign cavalry are in pursuit of our horsemen."

Ahmad glanced quickly in their direction.

"Aye," he replied, "but I doubt if they can reach the Betwa first."

The Rani's troop evidently perceived their danger for their horses were urged on to greater speed. Could the Betwa be reached they would be safe from further pursuit, but it was yet a good five miles distant.

Thus pursuers and pursued raced across the plain in full view of those watching from the fortress. The Foreign cavalry gained ground steadily in spite of the freshness of the others' horses.

"Ahmad," suddenly exclaimed the Rani, as if an idea had flashed upon her mind, "do thou go forth with my bodyguard and seek to draw off the Foreigners; but enter not into any rash engagement as we need every life in the defense of Jhansi. Hasten, good Ahmad, for Tantia Topi must not remain in doubt of our position."

Ahmad obediently hurried from her side, while the Rani anxiously awaited the outcome of her order.

Presently from the eastern gate she beheld Ahmad sweep forth at the head of a body of Valaiti troopers with the object of, in turn, cutting off the Foreign cavalry.

This the Foreigners quickly noticed and wheeled about to meet the new force.

The Rani clapped her hands joyfully, for the manœuvre enabled her flying mission to gain an unrecoverable advantage. She beheld them plunge to safety through the waters of the Betwa.

Those on the walls also watched the movement and cheered loudly upon its success.

In the gathering darkness Ahmad Khan then withdrew his detachment to the shelter of the walls.

A sleepless night was spent by those in authority within the threatened city. To a late hour the Rani sat in council discussing final plans for the defense. A mandate was issued calling upon every male able to bear arms to repair to the walls, and in her name, the Rani especially appealed to the women and children to render assistance, not in vain lamentations over the slain, but by carrying food and water to those unable to leave their posts.

At daybreak the enemy's cavalry was reported to have completely invested the city, and before night again came round, the main body of their army had arrived and were busily engaged erecting batteries from which to bombard the walls. It was evident their intention was to capture the entire garrison as well as the capital of the state.

A suggestion that the Rani should make her escape while there might yet remain an opportunity, was received by the fair defender with scorn.

"Fear not," she retorted with animation, "that I will suffer the indignity of capture at their hands. My dead body they may find, but the spirit of the Rani of Jhansi will have carried more than one of them to an accounting before the great tribunal of justice."

In two days the enemy's batteries were completed, then the storm of war burst with full violence upon the city. The garrison spiritedly returned the fire shot for shot with many to the good, breaches were made in the walls to be repaired by the hands of the women and children, animated to heroic actions by the presence and inspiring words of their beautiful queen, who seemed oblivious to any form of danger. At all hours she visited the ramparts to encourage her soldiers with stirring appeals.

Day by day, for seventeen in number, the duel of cannon shot was kept up on both sides, while watchers on the Jhansi citadel cast their vision with anxious eagerness across the Betwa to the north and west. Was Tantia Topi going to abandon them to the mercy of the Foreigners? The question forced itself upon their minds.

The situation was fast becoming desperate. Great rents had been made in the solid masonry at strategic points that could not be repaired. The dead and dying numbered hundreds. The besieged began to fight not with the hope of victory, but with the courage of despair.

At last the mamelon itself was reduced by the furious cannonade, its guns silenced. A hand to hand conflict seemed imminent. It was then the Rani performed an act of sublime courage which inspired admiration even in the eyes of her enemies.

Messenger after messenger had arrived at the palace bearing on their faces expressions of dismay that told without words of the terror seizing upon their hearts. One at length brought the worst news yet received.

"My Lady Rani," he spoke hurriedly. "The parapet of the mamelon is shot away, the breach momentarily widens, Ahmad Khan who, although badly wounded, still fights like ten thousand tigers, sends word that it must shortly be abandoned. Alas! the troops are becoming disheartened, and hesitate to obey their orders."

The spirit of the Rani rose upon the instant to confront the impending calamity.

"No," she cried, "the mamelon shall not be captured, while I have a voice to summon men to its defense."

She repaired quickly to her private apartments and

arrayed herself in magnificent attire so that in the act she contemplated there might be no doubt concerning her personality. Then she called for a horse and rode swiftly to the threatened spot.

As she approached the ramparts, evidences of the terrible devastation wrought by the shell of the enemy confronted her gaze. Broken walls, bodies horribly mangled where they had fallen, the forms of the mortally wounded writhing in their death agony, terrified faces cowering behind any shelter that could be obtained. A wide gap in the outworks of the mamelon proved that the fire of the besiegers had done effective work.

A feeble cheer greeted the Rani's arrival. She allowed it to pass unheeded. She dismounted, and without a moment's hesitation, strode fearlessly, past ghastly forms and over shattered blocks of masonry, toward the most exposed part of the walls.

Panic-stricken men turned their eyes upon her in wonder. A pulse of renewed courage began to throb in their hearts on beholding her presence among them. What was she about to do? they asked of each other in undertones.

Overhead the shot continued to rain a hail of destruction, but she pressed onward to the broken summit of the bastion. A shell struck the ground a few yards in advance, sending a cloud of dust into the air and scattering stones in all directions, but it did not cause her to swerve a foot from her path.

Ahmad Khan perceived her danger and hurried to her

side. His appearance told of the severity of the last few days of combat. One of his arms was suspended in a sling, his turbanless head bandaged to close the wound caused by the flying splinter of a rock, his stern visage dirt begrimed, his beard matted with congealed blood.

"Where goest thou, fair Rani"? he asked anxiously. "Turn back thy steps, I beg of thee. It is certain death to go forward."

She waved him back imperiously.

"I am not afraid," she cried above the din of the bombardment. "This scene is mine as a birthright. Did I not tell thee, I was a true Maratha."

He fell back and stumbled after her at a little distance.

She lightly passed over the remaining obstacles and mounted the broken parapet of the bastion. There in full view of the besiegers, in full range of their guns, she stood, a dauntless, defiant, superb figure of inspiring courage to all beholders. A gentle breeze played with her silken draperies. With a contemptuous smile she gazed serenely toward the enemy's battery. Fire, if you dare, seemed to be her challenge.

A gun that was quickly trained upon her could have instantaneously hurled her into oblivion, and thereby ended the siege of Jhansi. A soldier stood by it ready to fire at the officer's command. But the order did not come. To the credit of the chivalrous spirit of the Foreign general, he enjoined that yonder heroic girl should not suffer harm knowingly by his guns.

For several minutes she thus stood upon the threshold

of eternity, gazing calmly into its unfathomed depths; then turned and waved a hand encouragingly to those whose upturned faces regarded her safety in the daring act as an interposition of providence.

With a shout of renewed enthusiasm they rushed from their places of shelter to reman the abandoned fort. The roar of the bombardment rose higher than ever; but for the moment the city was saved from assault.

Chapter XVII

WITH SWORD AND TORCH

A GRAND salvo of artillery burst from the guns of the Jhansi fortress and was echoed by those of the other bastions as a joyful salute to the rising sun on that First of April. In the early light of dawn the sentries on the citadel had discerned far to the north-west the fluttering standards above the massed army of Tantia Topi marching to their relief. As it advanced across the Betwa the main body deployed into a long line of infantry, cavalry, and artillery, twenty thousand strong, with outspread wings to encircle the besieging army and crush it without affording a chance of retreat.

The gloom that on the night before had settled upon every face within the city, gave place to countenances transported with joy. The guns continued to thunder the glad news, bugles sounded their inspiriting notes, light hearts upon the walls gave expression to new hope by shouts of defiance to the enemy, and by bursting into the choruses of ancient war songs.

"The Foreigners are already beaten," they cried one to another, in accents of frenzied exultation. "Not one of them will escape."

But unfortunately for their own safety, they estimated the resource and courage of the enemy in a forlorn situation, at a computation that would have been their own under similar circumstances. The Foreigners were apparently not seized with a panic. Far otherwise, they seemed to be making preparations for a desperate fight. A victory for the Native army was not yet secured.

Early in the previous night the Rani had been informed of the welcome intelligence, and at daybreak had repaired to the citadel to watch the advancing host. She there called to a consultation her chief officers to discover the best means of assisting the Native general in his supreme effort to relieve the city.

After a careful survey of the situation, Ahmad urged the plan of sallying out in force at a critical moment of the forthcoming battle and attacking the rear of the Foreign army. It would undoubtedly throw their front line into confusion and accelerate the complete rout of their foes.

This was quickly acceded to by the others. The Rani was about to give an order for the collecting of the force near the eastern gate, when an unexpected development of the enemy's plan stayed the command.

The Foreign general instead of marching with his whole force to meet that of Tantia Topi, divided his command into two parts, one to continue the bombardment of the city, the other to give battle to the Native general in the open. To the amazement of those on the citadel they beheld a detachment of not more than fifteen hundred strong set out to combat a force over thirteen times superior in men, and almost as much more formidable in guns.

A sortie from the city was thus for the moment considered inadvisable, but the guns were ordered to return the fire of the besieging batteries with redoubled vigor. The men on the walls shouted and cheered to encourage the onward sweep of their deliverers.

From her elevated position the Rani anxiously watched the advance of the two forces toward each other, the result of which, though there could scarcely be any doubt, was fraught with so much consequence to herself. If the Foreigners were beaten and Jhansi relieved, the effect would be to enkindle the dying flames of the rebellion all over India. A long period must then elapse before Jhansi could again be threatened, if indeed the Foreigners would ever reappear before its walls.

But in the excitement of the momentous hour, other thoughts were not absent from her mind. With Tantia Topi was the sole object upon whom her real affection rested. A meeting between Prasad and herself would probably take place before the fall of night. What would be his manner toward her? How would she receive him? were questions to be answered. In the joy of victory it was probable that on her side his past cruelty would be forgiven, if not entirely swept from her memory. But would he have learned wisdom in his banishment? Would he better understand her nature and the difficulties of her position? That she loved him still in spite of his apparent worthlessness had never been a matter of doubt. She leaned her arms upon the parapet wondering over what part of the advancing army he would have been given the command.

Much time was not permitted for these reflections. The Foreign general instead of waiting to be attacked, threw consternation into both flanks of his foe by attacking those positions with his cavalry and horse artillery in impetuous onslaughts. The guns of both armies, added to those of the city bastions and besieging batteries, filled the air with smoke and the deafening sound of their discharges. It became difficult for those on the city walls to see clearly how the battle went. Still they cheered their friends on lustily.

Presently the roar of the cannon on the plain slackened. Were the Foreigners already vanquished the Rani hoped and wondered. Then the cloud of smoke rolled away disclosing to her appalled vision, not the Foreigners defeated, but the relieving army cast into inextricable confusion. Their wings had been doubled in upon the center at the moment that the Foreign infantry had attacked that vulnerable part, and the whole was being driven back upon the second line in a hopeless rout. The shouts of encouragement from the city walls ceased. It was perceived that the victory was not already won, but lost. No relief would come that day to the beleaguered garrison.

The Rani hastened to where her chiefs of staff were gathered. She besought them to lead a sortie to draw off the pursuing enemy. But they shook their heads despondingly. They pointed out that it would be a fruitless waste of life.

"If then there is not a soldier among you," she cried passionately. "I will lead it myself."

"Valiant Rani," petitioned Ahmad. "Surely thou wilt not accuse thy servant of cowardice, but it would be a rash, a hopeless act, unless yonder batteries were first silenced. Between them and the walls thy men would be mown down as grass."

She appeared to comprehend the force of his advice, though she stamped her foot and returned vehemently:

"If the day be lost, the Foreigners need not think that Jhansi hath been captured. Go you," she cried, "and see that rocks and trunks of trees are heaped about the walls, so that if an assault is made there shall be many broken skulls."

In the distance the Native army was retreating across the Betwa, but the Foreign cavalry kept mercilessly upon their heels. They set fire to the jungle to harass the pursuit, but amid the flames and smoke the fight continued. The retreat developed into a rout. Twenty thousand men fleeing before a less number of hundreds.

Presently the sun went down, a blood red orb for a moment resting on the horizon, ominous of the fate in store for those within the city.

On all sides dejected faces surrounded the Rani. Even Ahmad Khan maintained a gloomy silence in the despondency it was evident he felt. One officer even had the temerity to suggest a truce so that the enemy's terms might be learned.

The Rani flashed upon him a look of intense scorn.

"Not while I live," she cried, "hadst thou better do more than contemplate so cowardly an act. By Heaven! had I but officers possessed with daring like yonder Foreigners, they would not now be revelling in their victory. Nay, Jhansi would never have been attacked. In truth, I do not blame them for hanging all their prisoners. He who lives to fall into their hands well deserves that disgraceful fate. Surrender," she cried, "not while the Rani of Jhansi lives to teach you how to fight."

Their sense of honor was stung by the reproach.

Each swore loudly that he was prepared to die by her side.

"Aye, my Lords," she returned, "and I have in mind a plan that will strike amazement into the hearts of our enemies. Jhansi they shall never capture. I will first make of it the greatest funeral pyre that has ever blazed in India. It shall be even more sublime than that of Chitor, when thirteen thousand Hindu women, led by their Queen, cast themselves into a vast furnace, to save their honor from a conqueror."

"Go," she commanded to Ahmad, "and see that firewood is collected in houses in different parts of the town, and here in the palace. When the walls are carried, we will fire the city; when the palace is taken, it shall also be burned; and lastly, when the citadel can no longer hold out, the magazines shall be exploded; and the heavens and earth stand appalled at the last act of a Hindu woman defending her throne. Then let the Foreigners gather what plunder they may from the mound of ashes that was once the city of Jhansi. Truly history will record no more wondrous *johur*." [1]

The officers looked dumbfounded. Ahmad hesitated to execute the order.

"Go," she cried, stretching forth an arm impatiently. "It is my will. He who disobeys me at this hour is a traitor. With my own hand I will relieve the Foreigners of any vengeance on his account."

The officers left her presence marveling at her display of spirit and determination.

She turned to her waiting woman and bade her bring weapons from the palace armory.

"A dagger, I have, with the sharpest point ever yielded to a woman, but pistols, good Rati, and see to it they are well loaded; for perchance I shall be forced to take my own life out of the hands of these Foreigners."

The girl departed and left her mistress alone.

The Rani drew from her girdle Prasad's dagger, and gazed upon it thoughtfully.

"Keen is this blade," she murmured, "and relentless. Ah Prasad! How hath this day gone with thee, I wonder? Far hence our next meeting may be destined to take place. If living, I pray thou hast redeemed thine honor by a score of wounds. If dead, that thy body lies upon the field of battle."

[1] A last desperate general self sacrifice.

A quiver hovered about the corners of her lips. She hid the dagger in the folds of her *sari* gathered over her breast.

There was no question that the defensive power of the Jhansi garrison was reduced to the last extremity. They still manned the shattered walls, and massed about the breaches, but the place could not hold out for any length of time. One hope still remained. It was known that the Raja of Banpur had collected a force at Kotra within marching distance. To him, the Rani had dispatched overnight an urgent summons to come speedily to her assistance. But it was unknown if the messenger had been able to pass the enemy's lines.

Meanwhile, the elated Foreigners were making preparations for the final assault.

It was delivered at daybreak on the second morning after the defeat of the army of Tantia Topi.

Suddenly from positions of cover they dashed to those parts of the defenses leveled by the fire of their batteries. In the gray light of dawn bugles rang out on both sides calling men to a ruthless slaughter of each other. For a moment, a storm of bullets from the walls checked the Foreigners' onslaught. Then besiegers and besieged met in death earnest combat.

From the ramparts, missiles of all kinds were hurled upon the heads of those who strove to mount by ladders; through the breaches cannon shot, rockets, and volleys of musketry swept scores of the enemy into eternity.

Again and again repulsed they still fought their way onward.

At the part where the attack was directed by an attempt to scale the walls, the Rani encouraged both men and women defenders to invincible efforts. Ah God! how they fought with such inspiration. The ditch below was filled with the dead and dying. Groans called forth in return shouts of defiance. She still held the enemy at bay.

Had the assault at other points been as valiantly repulsed, victory might yet have rested with the besieged; but in the face of Foreign courage and Foreign bayonets they were beaten back. Thus the Rani found herself attacked in rear as well as in front. To defend the streets, the palace, and the citadel, in turn, went forth as the last order of the day.

As a consequence each house became a fort, in the capture of which no quarter was asked or given; every alley a stubbornly contested battlefield in miniature. The slain already numbered thousands.

At last the Foreigners fought their way to the vicinity of the palace, when, to their dismay, flames burst forth on either side throughout the length of the great bazaar. To retreat became impossible, to capture the palace a necessity.

They rushed forward across the open space, while a terrific fire from the guns of the citadel turned full upon them further decimated their ranks. With a supreme effort they battered down the doors to find every room, court, and corridor filled with desperate men, who sought death by the sword as a certain entry into Paradise. In the stables fifty Valaitis held out until the sun hid its face beneath the horizon, though the darkened heavens continued to reflect the angry glow of the burning city.

From the summit of the fortress, the Rani's banner still fluttered in the breeze. By force she had been carried into the citadel.

Her determination had been to perish on the steps of her throne. In the great hall, surrounded by her bodyguard, she stood to hurl a last defiance at her enemies, still unconquered, still resolute, in spite of the horrors she had witnessed. Every moment the din and tumult increased as the Foreigners fought their way to her position. While bronzed sinewy hands grasped their weapons, hers sought the dagger of her lover, lying near her heart.

From a side entrance Ahmad Khan, a dishevelled, conflict-stained object, rushed in, and without seeking her command, grasped her tightly by the arm. Her protest he heeded not, but drew her quickly to a door behind the throne, that opened into a narrow passage leading into the interior of the fortress. The guards closed in on her steps and swept her onward. In a few minutes she was in a place of temporary safety.

Thus night fell as a curtain to veil the scene of carnage.

Within a bare, stone walled room, the Rani had lain down upon a pile of mats, worn out with her exertions. On the floor near by a lamp cast a flickering light upon her features, that still displayed no sign of yielding. Food had been brought to her side by rough, though loving hands; but little of it had been partaken. For the hour, the silence of the visitation of death had succeeded the air-filled tumult of battle.

Presently the Rani turned her face to an officer standing near the door, and asked if Ahmad Khan was within call.

"He has been speaking with someone," the officer replied, "and now cometh this way."

In a moment Ahmad and a soldier entered the room.

"Good Ahmad," she asked. "How long dost think we can hold the citadel"?

"Noble Lady," he replied in a doubtful voice. "I fear not more than two or three days at most. The ammunition is well nigh exhausted; food and water are in scarce quantities. But this good fellow," he added, referring to the soldier, "brings a message from the foot of the rock, that a plan has been effected for your Highness's escape."

"Escape," the Rani cried contemptuously. "Hast thou not heard me vow a hundred times that I would perish with my people"?

"Aye," Ahmad acquiesced. "But, noble Rani," he urged, "I beg thou wilt listen to the best advice. Thy life and not thy death is of most advantage to the cause, bravely as all know thou wouldst yield the former. Tantia Topi now moves on Kalpi. Thy presence there is sorely needed. Below the rock, fathered in the shadow, are three hundred of thy remaining Valaiti troopers, together with a captain's escort from the force of Tantia Topi. The spot may be gained with a rope, and then fear not but that they will cut for thee a passage through a host of enemies. I do beg of thee not to hesitate a moment."

The Rani considered for a little, when it appeared as if she was about to fall in with his suggestion.

"But what will happen to these brave fellows, seemingly deserted in their hour of need"? she asked. "Does it not seem a craven act to abandon them to their fate"?

"Nay, brave Lady," Ahmad reasoned. "In thy flight lies the only safety for their lives. As long as thou art among them they will fight to the death; but when thou art gone they will surrender, and the Foreigners will show them mercy."

His argument evidently impressed the Rani favorably.

"True," she replied, "it would be a useless sacrifice. Besides, I may be able to persuade Tantia Topi to return to fight again for Jhansi. Are these troopers now in waiting"? she asked.

"In all anxiety for thy safety," he answered. "I do beg of thee not to lose a moment, for now that all the Foreigners are within the city there is little danger in thy path of flight. By daybreak it may be too late."

She hesitated a moment, then rose with her mind determined on the act. She drew a shawl over her face and shoulders as much to conceal her features as a protection from the night air.

"Lead quickly to the place," she enjoined, "or the sight of my brave soldiers may bring about a change of mind. I will bid them no farewell. I cannot, I dare not do so."

Through the darkness Ahmad conducted her rapidly to a part of the citadel wall, from which the descent to the plain though steep and hazardous was yet possible with the aid of a rope.

Without permitting her time for reflection, Ahmad secured one end of the rope under his arm pits, and holding her round the waist, swung down from the parapet. A soldier above slowly paid out the rope as Ahmad directed by pre-arranged signals. More than once it strained and quivered with their weight, several times his feet slid from the ledges of rock upon which they momentarily rested. Above their heads the fortress loomed a huge black mass; below their feet there fell away an impenetrable abyss. The well-feigned cry of a night bird announced to those below that the fugitives had left the fortress. In response, there rose the howl of a jackal.

Presently, it seemed an hour had passed, a familiar voice fell upon the Rani's ears. There was no time permitted to ask its owner's name, for a pair of stout arms relieved Ahmad of his burden, and she found herself placed on the saddle of a horse.

Ahmad quickly disengaged himself from the rope and sprang on to another waiting mount, the cry of the jackal again rose as a signal that the feat had been safely accomplished, and thus shielded by the swords of her devoted troopers, the Rani commenced the second stage of her escape.

On the morrow, the citadel surrendered to terms; and the blind beggar crept forth from his hiding place to resume his seat in the shade by the palace doors.

Chapter XVIII

A PRINCE IN SCARLET

WITH caution, the troopers encircling the Rani, felt their way out from the shadow of the rock. Then with loosened reins they rode, as with the speed of a monsoon wind, northward to the rendezvous of the Native forces at Kalpi.

At first, they avoided the main road and, with unslackened pace, took to by-paths that led over ditches and streams, through dense jungle underbrush, and across rocky plains, until the danger of an immediate pursuit was past. Throughout the night the form of the officer who had taken the Rani from Ahmad's arms kept closely at her side. That his order must have been to watch over her as a priceless treasure, was evident from the care he took to guide her horse at dangerous places, and to remove from her course an occasional overhanging branch that might have caused painful if not serious injury. In the darkness his features were indistinguishable. Indeed, it seemed as if he purposely kept his face turned from her; though in the open, the brilliancy of the starlight shining upon a closely fitting cap of steel, and arms of ornate workmanship, proclaimed him a cavalier of rank.

As in the early part of the ride silence was imperative, the Rani did not attempt to broach a conversation with her companion. In fact, the pace was too swift to permit even a consecutive flow of thought. Such thoughts as did occupy her mind were naturally directed to the reasons she would urge upon Tantia Topi for the immediate recapture of her beloved city.

Day was breaking when the troopers drew up before the fortress gates of a friendly raja. The Rani glanced round to offer her thanks to the officer who had so faithfully protected her from harm during the long night ride; but he had disappeared. So also had Ahmad Khan.

Upon seeking the reason for their absence, she was informed that on striking into the main road, the former had fallen behind with a small body of men to cover her retreat, and the latter had been compelled to seek relief from his fatigue by a short period of rest in the seclusion of the jungle.

A sudden inspiration prompted her to ask the name of the gallant captain of the escort. A look of disappointment crossed her face upon learning that he was a northern chief attached to the army of Tantia Topi, by name, Parma Nand Bai Bahadur.

It seemed to the Rani that she had scarcely closed her eyes in much needed sleep, when a trooper arrived in haste bearing the waking message that the Foreign cavalry were in pursuit.

"To the saddle," was the immediate cry. Within a few minutes she was again flying northward, her escort reinforced by the presence and body-guard of her recent host.

Through the trying heat of day, with but momentary halts for refreshment, she pressed forward over the hundred and ten miles intervening between Jhansi and Kalpi. At nightfall a trooper caught up with her party to deliver the welcome intelligence that the rearguard had beheld the Foreign cavalry relinquish the pursuit.

Thus she was enabled to rest for the night at a wayside village without fear of personal danger. Before retiring, and again on setting forth the next morning she had looked for the reappearance of the officer who had so skillfully conducted her retreat; but it seemed he had turned back upon the heels of the Foreign cavalry to make certain of their actions.

By easier stages she accomplished the remaining distance to Kalpi, reaching her destination at sunset to find that she had outstripped Tantia Topi in his more leisurely retreat from Jhansi. In the waning light his vanguard was seen emerging from the ravines by which the city is approached on three sides. On its fourth, the sacred waters of the Jumna reflected the deep shadows of a long line of temples and mausoleums, terminating in the rock fortress with the *ghat* at its foot.

The Rao Sahib, who, as the nephew and representative of the Peshwa, had for several months commanded the garrison and arsenal at Kalpi, was advised of the Rani's approach. He sent forward an aide-de-camp to meet her on the road, and with greetings conduct her to a house prepared for her reception. He requested that early on the following morning she would assist at a council-of-war to discuss the operations necessary to turn back the victorious advance of the enemy.

The Rani was concluding her evening meal, when raising her eyes they rested with surprise upon the form of her worthy secretary, Bipin Dat.

"Why, good Bipin," she exclaimed in accents of welcome. "Thou here. I thought thou wert far off discussing intricate family problems with thy genial uncles."

"Illustrious Lady," Bipin replied gravely. "Such was undoubtedly my intention when I departed from your Highness's side in Jhansi; but alas! the pace of those rascally troopers thou gavest me as an escort, so jolted my limbs, that on reaching the camp of the invincible Tantia Topi, I could scarce crawl into his presence. For days my bones ached to such an extent that a tortoise would have travelled faster to the abode of my people. Then when I learned the straits in which your Greatness was placed, how could I do otherwise than assist in your relief."

"I see," the Rani exclaimed. "Thy aches and pains vanished when it became necessary to move faster than a tortoise, after that feat was so gallantly relinquished."

"Noble Rani," protested Bipin. "Had the great Tantia Topi only followed the advice of thy humble servant and been more circumspect in his method of attack, undoubtedly the Foreigners would all have been eaten up like grass before a plague of locusts. As it was, with several other observant fellows, I saw to it that no assault was contemplated in rear while the battle raged in front—a responsible office, great Lady," he concluded, self approvingly, "that Tantia Topi admitted had been well carried out."

"No doubt," acquiesced the Rani, expressing in her voice the contempt she felt for the conduct of those in command of the Native army on that critical occasion. "No doubt, good Bipin. The retreat, they say, was conducted with masterly judgment. But tell me," she asked with greater interest. "Hast thou seen aught of Prasad Singh with the army of Tantia Topi"?

Bipin started at the mention of the Hindu noble's name.

"Thanks be to God, not I," he exclaimed. "By the will of the Almighty I trust his spirit has long since passed into the body of a toad. I have seen naught of that accursed man."

The Rani's brow darkened for a moment as if Bipin's expression of sentiment met with her disapproval; but she spoke again in reference to another matter.

"Good Bipin," she said, "I am glad to see thee once more, for thou canst render me an immediate service."

He *salaamed* obediently, while she took a purse from her girdle and handed him a considerable sum of money.

"Go," she enjoined, "into the bazaar, and without disclosing who it is that commissions thee, purchase for me a suit of male attire. I would have thee buy a scarlet jacket and trousers, a white turban, and red leather shoes to which spurs may be strapped. Get me also a sword of the finest tempered steel, and pistols that will shoot straight. Remember I care more for the quality of the weapons than for their ornamentation. Let it be understood that the sword and pistols will be purchased only if they meet with my approval. Thou hadst better order several from which I can make a choice. Go, and do this speedily, as I have a use for them upon the morrow."

With an expression of surprise on his face Bipin hesitated, when the Rani, emphatically repeating her order, he *salaamed* and departed on his errand.

The sun had risen but a few degrees above the horizon on the following morning when the Rao Sahib, Tantia Topi, Ahmad Khan, who had arrived in Kalpi overnight, and other native leaders, were gathered about a table in a room of the governor's house, awaiting the Rani of Jhansi's coming to take a seat at the council.

A curtain screening the doorway of the room was drawn aside and a young officer entered. With the exception of his white turban, he was attired in a blood red uniform from head to foot. It contrasted well with his dark, handsome features, and admirably displayed his slender figure. One hand, unusually delicate for a man, rested upon the butt of a pistol protruding from his girdle, while the other rose to his turban in a military salute.

The Rao Sahib and Tantia Topi gazed inquiringly as well as with admiration, upon the newcomer, whom it was evident they had never seen before. Ahmad Khan with his back to the stranger's position had failed to remark his entrance.

With the exception of a white turban, she was attired in a blood-red uniform from head to foot.—Page 213.

"Well officer," the Rao Sahib asked. "Dost bring us a message from someone"?

The young officer laughed musically as he assumed a captivating pose.

"I bring you a message, noble Sahibs," he replied, "to say that the Raja of Jhansi is now present at the council."

"The Raja of Jhansi"? the Rao Sahib and Tantia Topi both echoed interrogatively, while Ahmad turned impulsively in his seat.

For a moment the Mohammedan scrutinized the young officer's features, then gave vent to an exclamation of surprise.

"By Allah"! he cried, "my Lords, it is the valiant Rani herself."

The nobles rose from their seats and welcomed her effusively. For a space the eyes of the Rao Sahib could discover no other object save her form to gaze upon.

She gracefully moved forward and took a seat at the board. The cloud of misfortune that had overshadowed their faces was lifted by her presence. As a ray of heaven's light to storm-beset travellers she came among them.

For a time the assembled nobles proceeded to discuss the events leading up to the numerous reverses they had recently suffered, those more directly implicated endeavoring by one plea and another to shirk individual responsibility. In this useless wrangle over past disasters the Rani's patience soon became exhausted. She perceived that unless brought to a speedy termination it might lead, by way of heated arguments, to the greater disaster of a feud among themselves. Already Ahmad Khan and Tantia Topi had exchanged angry words over the generalship displayed in the battle before Jhansi.

"My Lords," she at this point interposed. "All this seems to me to add little to the solution of our present difficulty, except in so far as we may have gathered experience to bring victory out of defeat. With deference to your greater knowledge of such matters, in my mind the most important question, is how to insure a speedy turn of the campaign in our favor."

"Truly, thou speakest to the point, O Rani," the Rao Sahib remarked approvingly. "Dost agree then with Tantia Topi, that we intrench ourselves here in Kalpi and await the coming of the Foreigners"?

The Rani rose to her feet with a gesture of impatience.

"Noble Rao," she returned vehemently. "That plan will never do. If it was impossible to hold Jhansi, a stronger position by a hundred fold than any that might be afforded by the defenses here, how do you suppose we could drive away the Foreigners from Kalpi? No," she urged, "while I agree that the Kalpi arsenal must be saved to us at all costs, I believe that the enemy must first be fought and beaten in the open, at a time and place the most advantageous to ourselves. To a spot of our own selection, I would move forward to encounter them on their way from Jhansi. There, with our troops well rested and theirs exhausted by a long march, the chance of victory will rest on our side. Aye, I would so arrange the hour of battle that we fight in the heat of noonday, when the sun will aid us as a powerful ally."

"Well spoken, brave Rani," Ahmad Khan applauded enthusiastically. "Hadst thou learned thy military lessons from the great Dost Mohammed, thou couldst not have counseled us more wisely."

"Nay, my lords," she protested, "it is after all but the opinion of a woman; but if any remain still in doubt as to the advisability of the plan, give into my hands the command of this affair and see what comes of it. If a leader's courage can drive these people back, I vow they shall never desecrate with their feet the eighty temples of Kalpi."

The Rao Sahib was enthralled by the beauty and enthusiasm of the Rani of Jhansi. He would willingly have granted her request, but that he was fearful of offending the susceptibilities of his generals. He pondered deeply before rendering a decision. At last he spoke authoritatively.

"In what the Rani says there is certainly displayed much good discernment of the situation. I agree with her that it is better to intercept the Foreigners' advance than await them here in Kalpi. So if she will accept the leadership of the cavalry under the supreme command of Tantia Topi, I believe Kalpi may be saved."

"Noble Rao Sahib," the Rani returned. "Most readily will I accept any office which you may be pleased to give into my hands. But I would urge that we set out forthwith, in order that we may have time to select a good position. Be assured the Foreigners will not rest while another prize remains to fall into their hands."

"Thou art right, noble Rani," the Rao Sahib acquiesced. Then turning to Tantia Topi he asked if any place suggested itself to his mind as the best vantage ground on which to meet the enemy.

Tantia Topi called for a map of the country, and for several minutes studied it carefully. At last he gave it as his opinion that at Kunch, forty miles distant, the nature of the country would afford the best strategic position for a decisive battle.

"It is a good place," he explained, "because lying half way on the road to Jhansi, if the rout of the Foreigners be complete, a flying column may push swiftly on to the Rani's capital, with a chance of surprising and capturing the weak garrison that the Foreign general can only afford to leave there."

"Good, most sagacious Tantia Topi," the Rani exclaimed approvingly. Then turning to the Rao Sahib she earnestly besought of him a favor.

"My Lord," she said, "thou wilt not deny me the command of any force detached for the recapture of my own city"?

The Rao Sahib replied with gallantry.

"Assuredly that thou shalt possess, fair cavalier. Tantia Topi now hath my orders to give that command to no one else.

"So to Kunch, my Lords," he added, "is our final decision."

"Aye and to victory, forget not that," the Rani cried enthusiastically.

The council then proceeded with a discussion of the details of the expedition, to rise, at last, confident that with the greater number of men and guns they could put into the field, together with natural advantages on their side, the result of the battle could not be otherwise than a victory for the Native arms.

Chapter XIX

A CALL TO THE HEART

NEAR the decaying town of Kunch the Native army had taken up a strong position. In the shelter of woods and gardens, interspersed here and there with temples, for the time being occupied as miniature forts, the whole was fronted by a high wall over which a row of cannon peered their sinister muzzles.

For several days the retainers of numerous petty rajas, driven back upon the main body by the advance of the enemy, had been arriving to reinforce those who confidently believed they were about to deliver a death blow to the Foreigners. The plan of battle had been skillfully arranged. Under the supreme direction of Tantia Topi, Ahmad Khan had been given the command of the artillery, the Rani of Jhansi the cavalry, and Parma Nand Rai Bahadur, the officer who had rescued the Rani from Jhansi, and who purposely or otherwise managed to keep personally out of view, the duty of remaining in touch with the vanguard of the foe. If the attack was made at daybreak, the order was to hold the enemy at bay until the sun had climbed high into the meridian, and then with the whole force deliver a counter assault that, in the terrific heat of noon, must take the enemy at the greatest disadvantage. It was with eager expectancy that both leaders and men of the Native army awaited the battle that was to crush the power of the Foreigners in the central provinces of India. All was in readiness; only one element of doubt as yet remained undetermined—that the Foreigners would fall in with the plans made for their destruction.

It was early on a May morning that scouts brought in the intelligence that the enemy was in sight of Kunch.

The various arms took up their positions immediately. On the right, a little in the rear of the infantry, the Rani of Jhansi galloped to the head of her command and addressed to her men a few well chosen words of encouragement.

In response they cheered lustily, as they waved their swords in the bright sunshine.

"We will follow thee to the death, O valiant Rani," they shouted enthusiastically.

Of a truth, in both armies, there was on that day no more gallant or inspiring figure than that of the girl in the scarlet uniform. From her white turban there rose and flashed a diamond aigrette, a parting gift of good fortune from the Rao Sahib, who had remained at Kalpi. He, too, now regarded himself as an aspirant to her tender favor.

Thus the men stood to their arms watching a running skirmish over the plain between their outposts and what was believed to be the vanguard of the enemy, when a terrible fusilade of musketry and artillery fire burst upon their unprotected left flank and rear.

The enemy had not fallen in with the plans for their destruction, but with Occidental perversity had consummated others of their own. The bulk of the Foreign army had, overnight, made a wide detour unobserved, and was now perilously threatening the Native force's line of retreat—a movement, that the Foreign general knew from experience, the Native commanders would be unable to view with any other feeling than dread. By this action the battle was won for the Foreigners before it had even commenced.

Tantia Topi cast a single terrified glance over the field and fled precipitately; but Ahmad Khan quickly grasped the situation, in so far as his own branch of the service was concerned. If he could only bring his guns to bear upon the force advancing from the unexpected direction, the Foreigners might be held in check until order was restored out of the panic that prevailed. The infantry deserted by their leader had become unmanageable, but the Rani of Jhansi still held the cavalry together awaiting orders. To her, Ahmad dispatched an urgent message begging her to cover his contemplated movement.

She was about to respond promptly, when, glancing backward she noticed a picket that had been driven in by the enemy engaged in a desperate encounter with a larger body of cavalry. In the centre, fighting for his life with no hope of escape, she beheld the form of the officer who had succeeded in effecting her deliverance from Jhansi. The *mêlée* was too far distant to discern his features, but intuitively, without a hesitating doubt, she knew that Parma Nand Rai Bahadur was one with Prasad Singh.

Ahmad's request, the peril of the Native army, both were swept from her mind in the face of her lover's danger. Without another thought than for his safety, she gave no order, but impulsively spurred her horse at a broken part of the intervening wall, and dashed to his rescue. Her command, not understanding what course to pursue, divided of their own volition into two parties, the Valaiti troopers following their mistress, the rest galloping after the infantry in retreat. Thus Ahmad Khan, muttering all the curses in his vocabulary, was left to extricate himself as best he could.

With uplifted sword the Rani came down upon the Foreign cavalry like an avenging spirit. At last she was hand to hand with them. Three Native troopers of the enemy she hurled groaning to the dust. Right and left she gallantly parried and delivered blows. Her Valaitis closed about her, as she cut her way toward her lover's side.

Prasad's horse had fallen. On foot he was fighting despairingly when her image rose before his eyes, superbly animated with the ardor of mortal combat.

"Prasad! Prasad!" she cried. "The Rani of Jhansi cometh to thee."

She raised her sword to parry a blow delivered at his head, but her hand dropped lifelessly to her side. The scene became a hazy blur in her vision, reeling in her saddle she lost consciousness. When she regained her senses she was far from the battlefield of Kunch.

The victory of the Foreigners had again been complete. The retreat of the Native army, at first conducted with order, finally developed into a rout, in which the Valaitis swiftly bore the Rani back to Kalpi. The Rao Sahib seized with the same panic that had carried Tantia Topi from the field to an unknown destination, quickly left Kalpi to its fate. In the city all was confusion. The infantry vowed they had been abandoned by the artillery; the artillery, through the mouth of Ahmad Khan, swore that the cavalry had deserted them at the critical moment and thereby lost the battle. Without a leader, the bulk of the troops were seeking individual safety in the jungles. They believed the enemy was upon their heels.

Such was the situation to which the Rani opened her eyes, on recovering from the glancing blow that had placed her temporarily *hors de combat*.

Her first thoughts were of Prasad. She inquired anxiously of those about her if any news of him had been obtained. The answer was in part satisfactory. He had been seen during the flight from Kunch, and was believed to have been ordered to escort Tantia Topi to a place of safety.

The Rani rose from her couch to view with silent contempt and outspoken denunciation the craven spirit that had captured all who remained in Kalpi.

"The Foreigners are upon us," they replied to her

entreaties to make a last stand at Kalpi. "We cannot fight against them. They will kill all the prisoners. It is better to fly while there is time."

At this juncture news was brought to the Rani that the Nawab of Bandah had arrived before Kalpi with a considerable force. The Rani hastened to his presence, and besought him in fervent language to save the only arsenal in their hands. But the Nawab of Bandah had just suffered a defeat himself. He had trusted to share in the triumph of the Rao Sahib after Kunch. He certainly had no stomach to become the hero of a forlorn hope. Under the circumstances he was much more inclined to discuss the safest place of retreat.

In despair of being able to induce him to accede to her purpose, the Rani was forced to summon Ahmad Khan to her aid, at a moment when the Mohammedan's humor was deeply offended by her conduct at Kunch.

"Ah," he returned sarcastically. "The brave Rani is anxious enough to avail herself of Ahmad's services when it suits her convenience; but when he has fallen into a ditch, he might summon the moon to his relief with a surer hope of response."

"Nay, good Ahmad," the Rani replied winningly, "truly I did not realize thou wert in such distress. I only saw the desperate need of assistance in which Bai Bahadur was placed."

"To be sure," he answered tersely. "And who may be this Bai Bahadur"?

"Thou knowest as much of him as I," the Rani replied. "But, good Ahmad," she pleaded, "thou wilt, I know, support me with this Nawab"?

"Assuredly," he acquiesced in a yielding tone. "Thou hast a power with us, fair Rani, to gain an end possessed by no other. Verily, such an obedient hound am I at the sound of thy voice, that I believe if thou wert to order me to go forth as a *yogi* and sit at thy door for the rest of my days blinking at the sun, the eternal damnation of the Prophet would not stay my following thy command. What wouldst thou have me do with this Bandah Nawab"? he asked.

The Rani explained the Nawab's faintheartedness and suggested that Ahmad might use a little of the persuasion so effectual with Sadescheo.

"Aye," he replied twirling his moustaches fiercely. "But say the word, fair Lady, and for thy sake I will persuade my hand to cut his head off as the beginning of my argument."

"Let it be not quite so demonstrative," she enjoined. "But I would have thee be emphatic none the less."

"The battle yell of thy Valaitis will sound as a love ditty in his ears afterwards," he returned, and continued. "Thou art determined then to meet the Foreigners again"?

"Aye," she replied with spirit, "and to continue meeting them until I have won a victory or perished in the attempt."

The result of Ahmad Khan's conference with the Bandah Nawab was a prompt decision to make a last endeavor to save Kalpi. As a fortress to withstand a siege it was indefensible, but the ravines and ridges surrounding the city afforded the best field for intrenched positions. By day and night, under the supervision of the Rani and Ahmad Khan, men labored indefatigably upon these works, momentarily expecting the appearance of the enemy.

But the Foreigners were completely exhausted by the difficulties of the long march to Kunch, and the subsequent battle. It was impossible to follow up the retreat of the Native army and seize upon Kalpi before discipline could be restored in the defender's ranks. By short marches only could they advance further, to find that the girl whom they had come to regard as the soul of the rebellion in Central India, was ready to meet them in a more desperate resistance than ever. The Foreign general realized speedily that she had rendered her position well nigh impregnable.

The Rani was not of the temper to await an attack from behind earthworks, with ever one eye on her line of retreat. She took the supreme command into her own hands, and so harassed the Foreigners' advance with her cavalry, that when they beheld the labyrinth of defenses raised as if by magic, on the three vulnerable sides of the town, they did not contemplate a retrograde movement, but a victory seemed more than doubtful. For both sides the day of another decisive battle was at hand.

In the meantime the Rao Sahib had heard of the successful efforts of the Rani to bring order out of chaos in the demoralized condition of the Native army after Kunch. He returned to reap the reward of a more than probable victory, and as a consequence the supreme command again reverted to his hands. At a council of war before the battle he was not unmindful of escape in case of defeat.

"We can cross the river and plunge into the jungles in that event," he remarked. "The Foreigners will not follow us into those recesses."

Scorn, anger, in a sense despair, were mingled in the Rani's voice, as with burning cheeks and flashing eyes she retorted hotly.

"Escape, my lords," she cried, "if we only set as little store upon escape as do these Foreigners, not one of them would now remain in India."

She rose abruptly and strode without further utterance from the council.

"A beautiful woman, a wonderful woman, with an accursed Afghan lion in leash at her side," remarked the Nawab of Bandah; "but noble Rao Sahib, thou dost well nevertheless to look to it, that we are not caught here in a trap."

Unfortunately for the Native army that sentiment dominated all their actions. It was the weight that turned the scale of battle in favor of the Foreigners at Jhansi, at Kunch, and lastly at Kalpi.

When the first onslaught came, the Native army repulsed the Foreigners with desperate valor. The sun again aided their efforts and decimated the enemy's ranks as much with blasts of heat as did the storm of shot and shell, poured forth in a blaze of fire from every ridge upon which the attack was directed. The odds were too great against the Foreigners. They wavered.

In a ravine, the Rani held the cavalry in waiting for such a turning point of the battle. She quickly noticed the reaction, and with a cheer, caught up by the whole body of her command, dashed upon the dismayed Foreigners. For a moment the battle seemed to be won, but only for a moment.

While she was engaged driving back the frontal attack, with ruthless slaughter on both sides, the Foreign general had succeeded in again effecting a flank movement threatening his enemy's retreat.

The Rao Sahib and the Nawab of Bandah cast a despairing look across the river to the jungles beyond, hesitated when they should have led all their forces forward; a shell burst near them; they turned their horses' heads and fled.

Meanwhile the Rani, flushed with victory, was still driving her opposing force before her, when glancing backward she beheld with a sinking heart the Native army in full retreat. A cheer from the Foreigners announced too plainly that for her, the day was lost.

"The cowards," she muttered, as tears of passionate

grief coursed down her cheeks. "Oh, the cowards! Will nothing stimulate their courage"?

With valor born of desperation she hurled herself upon the enemy still in front and cut her way between their ranks. Once more surrounded by her faithful Valaitis she was compelled to fly, on this occasion to the shelter of the jungle.

Chapter XX

BIPIN TAKES A PRISONER

WHEN the first messenger from Kunch rode into Kalpi, as if a thousand demons were in pursuit, shouting wildly that the day was lost; the worthy secretary, Bipin Dat, bitterly reproached himself for not having, at all hazards, continued his journey to the abode of his family. "*Ah, hae, hae*"! he groaned, "what God is unappeased by which a peaceful man is continually involved in these affairs of bloodshed. This all comes of not consulting an astrologer before setting out from Jhansi. He might have so arranged matters with the heavens, that a whirlwind would have scattered the Foreigners. Unfortunate is it, that the great Rani sets so little faith in the all powerful astrologers."

He quickly gathered a few trinkets together, carefully secreted them in the folds of his turban, and was among the earliest to plunge into the jungle.

There, for several days he wandered about in fear of wild beasts, of robbers, and of evil spirits. In what direction his footsteps were bent, he had but a faint idea; his sole aim being to place between himself and the scene of hostilities the greatest possible distance. An occasional hut afforded him a sleeping place, where, in the universal charity displayed to travellers, he was provided gratuitously with such meagre fare as could be offered.

How far he had wandered, Bipin could make no computation. The people of the jungle knew only of their immediate neighborhood. It seemed to him he must have travelled a great distance. In reality, like many under similar circumstances, he had been rambling in circles. At the end of two weeks he was still within thirty miles of the place he was eager to view from a distance of two hundred.

The day's tramp had been more than usually a toilsome one for Bipin. He had taken a narrow path that seemed to wander capriciously amid tangled underbrush with no particular destination. The sun had set without a village or habitation in sight, and the mysterious silence of the jungle, its ominous shadows, its majestic gloom, filled his soul with dread. He was reluctant to go forward, afraid to remain on the spot, and hesitated to turn back. His terrified fancy beheld the eyes of a panther or a tiger glaring out at him from behind every bush. The breaking of a twig, the sound of his own footsteps startled him nearly out of his senses. Thrice that day had a fox crossed his path, the worst possible omen. He beat his breast in his wretchedness. In turn, his fat cheeks and brow became flushed, and chill as the damp slab of a tomb.

"Oh, what a fool have I been," he groaned, "to mix my life up in the intrigues and ambitions of a court. How much better had I only remained in my humble condition with my good uncles. I would never have come to this unlucky pass."

BIPIN TAKES A PRISONER

Before him the path made a bend. Through the branches he thought he discerned a flickering light. It might come from a hut, or, he shivered, from the watch fire of a detachment of the Foreigners. In the morning he had heard that parties of them were beating the jungle for fugitives.

But in his deplorable situation, he reasoned, that it would be better to fall into their hands with the chance of being able to prove his innocence of rebellion, than remain where he was, a prey to some malign influence that, for all he knew to the contrary, might change him into a bat. He gathered his tattered garments about him, and moved cautiously toward the light. He had not taken many steps when a hand stretched out from the darkness laid a firm grasp upon his shoulder. At the same moment a voice in his own language gruffly called on him to halt.

"Who art thou, and whitherward"?

Bipin cast his arms above his head despairingly. His challenger might be a robber, or the Native sentry of a Foreign encampment.

"But a poor traveller—a devotee on his way to the holy river," he cried timorously, "a man of peace seeking a shelter for the night."

It was a fortunate inspiration that prompted him to pose as a pilgrim to the bank of the holy Ganges. The vilest malefactor would respect the sanctity of his person undergoing such a pious obligation. Had the idea only occurred to him before, it would have saved many qualms of nervous emotion. The accursed fox would have fled precipitately at the cry of "*Ganga! Ganga*"!

To Bipin's relief his captor replied in friendly accents:

"Why, surely. thy voice is not unknown to my ears. Art thou not one of the Rani of Jhansi's attendants"?

Bipin was about to vow by all his Gods that so far from being in any sympathy with the Native army, he detested their actions and loved the Foreigners as his uncles. For a moment he was tempted to declare, that never in his life had he beheld the face of the great Princess, and reassert more firmly his sacred mission; when it occurred to him that he might have stumbled upon a detachment of the fleeing Native army. He promptly decided to make sure of this point before committing himself to a confounding statement.

"And thy voice, too, I seem to know," he returned. "Art thou not also one of her followers"?

"A servant of the valiant Rani, herself," came the terse response.

"Blessed Devi," cried Bipin joyfully. "Am I not her worthy secretary, Bipin Dat. Tell me, good fellow, where I may discover her Highness, for whom I have been vainly searching in the jungle these many days past."

"That is easily done, holy pilgrim," replied the other, with a laugh, at the secretary's sudden change of garment. "She is encamped here with a body of her Valaitis, in retreat from Kalpi. Come, I will take thee to her presence."

BIPIN TAKES A PRISONER

The sentry led Bipin a short distance to an open space in which two or three hundred Valaitis were resting with their horses tethered at hand. Near a small camp fire the Rani was seated gazing pensively into the smouldering embers, kept purposely from rising into a blaze for fear of disclosing her place of concealment. She did not notice Bipin's approach until he had prostrated himself at her feet. Then she turned her eyes upon him without speaking.

"Great Rani," he at last exclaimed. "Behold thy worthy servant, Bipin Dat."

"Aye," she replied gravely but not unkindly. "Thou art a strange creature, appearing where least expected. Better would it have been for thee, good Bipin, if thou hadst taken another road than that which led to the Rani's camp. I would urge thee to seek speedily thy home, for with us henceforth there will be little use for thy pen."

A note of sadness in her voice appealed to a sympathetic chord even in the timorous nature of her secretary. It reproached him with cowardice and infidelity to his beautiful, heroic mistress.

"Lovely Rani," he cried penitently. "I vow hereafter I will never leave thy side, come good or evil fortune."

"Bipin," she replied with lighter spirit. "Though the present hour is dark enough, it may yet be that those who follow me shall bask in the brightest sunshine. If thou art determined to be among them, thou hadst better seek thy rest, for by daybreak we must be far hence."

A prudent man, the worthy secretary took a careful survey of the camp before deciding on his sleeping place. Not that there was much choice as regards a comfortable position. It was the bare ground for both the Rani and her attendants; but in his turban there were still hidden certain articles of value that might tempt the cupidity of the Valaiti troopers. If in guarding his sleep they despoiled him of his remaining possessions, he reasoned, that he would have paid overmuch for a night's security.

In this dilemma, his eyes chanced to observe the well spreading branches of a tree, under which the Rani had taken up a reclining position. They suggested to him a safe retreat. With some difficulty he climbed the lower trunk and discovered a spot that nature might have constructed to suit his present need. He curled himself up where two stout limbs branched off into space, and amid the shelter of the foliage was soon fast asleep.

The silence of midnight descended on the camp, the fire died low, an occasional grunt from the throat of a heavy sleeping trooper on the ground, and a sonorous gurgle from that of the secretary aloft, were the only noises distinguishable to the sentries.

Presently the worthy secretary began to dream of the peaceful abode of his uncles. It was a soothing picture to his troubled mind, but unfortunately, like the reality of life, it was not destined to last long without a counterpart of woe. In that absurdly impossible procedure of dreams, the accursed barber of Jhansi appeared on the scene, attired for all the world like a Foreign soldier—

in fact, a horrible nightmare, dual personality, endeavoring to shave off Bipin's nose and ears with a two handed sword of immense proportions. In his sleep the secretary struggled and gasped, for it seemed that the barber-soldier had seized him by the throat and was endeavoring to choke the breath out of his lungs. Indeed, the choking sensation became so terribly realistic, that he awoke with a wail of anguish to find that it was no dream at all, but that some huge, black monster, manlike so far as he could discern its face in the darkness, had grasped him round the neck, probably with the object of murdering him for the treasures concealed in his turban.

"Thieves! Murder! The Foreigners"! shouted Bipin, as loudly as the little wind left in his chest would permit. He entwined his legs and arms about a furry body and commenced a struggle for his life.

At Bipin's cry of "The Foreigners," the camp was instantly aroused. Horses neighed and pawed the earth, the troopers sprang to their feet, the sentries rushed in and stood gazing up into the tree from which there came a medley of strange noises. From the tumult, and the shower of twigs and leaves that fell upon their upturned faces, it was evident a desperate conflict was proceeding.

"The Foreigners! Thieves! The accursed Foreigners. To the rescue, brave Rani; oh! to the rescue, good comrades," the voice of Bipin saluted their astonished ears. Then came screams and chattering in an unknown tongue, with a fiercer renewal of the unseen combat.

The Rani had been awakened with the rest. She was

about to order some of the men to climb up into the tree and discover the nature of the disturbance, when, with a crashing of branches, a struggling black mass fell into their midst.

The troopers started back and then returned to separate the combatants that still writhed and fought upon the ground, when the form of Bipin struggled to his feet. He grasped a hairy baboon by the neck, and held him a captive before the Rani.

"Ah, what a ruffian," he panted, "to attempt to strangle me in my sleep. Without doubt he must embody the spirit of some wicked enemy."

In spite of her overshadowing misfortune, the Rani could not restrain a laugh at the humor of the situation.

"Thou art a brave fellow," she exclaimed, "and hast earned thy right to fight with a lance instead of a pen. Some day, perchance, thou wilt command a troop."

"Truly," reflected Bipin, "whether I like it or no, Fate will have it that I am to be mixed up continually in some accursed broil. If not with men, alas! it seems with the animals. Such is the inscrutable will of God."

The troopers' voices echoed the Rani's sally with laughter. They drove the baboon from the camp, peace was restored, slumber once more descended upon their heads. Before daybreak the party were speeding in a southwesterly direction toward a rendezvous of the Native chiefs at Gopalpur.

Chapter XXI

THE GREAT COUP DE MAIN

IT was but a fragment of the army defeated at Kalpi that had gathered within the insecure walls of Gopalpur.

Of the leaders, the Rao Sahib and Ahmad Khan had preceded the Rani of Jhansi to that place. Tantia Topi and Rai Bahadur or Prasad Singh, were hourly expected. Upon their arrival a council was summoned to decide what was best to be done in the hopeless strait to which the Native cause was reduced. To the North, East, and South; in whichever direction their gaze turned, they beheld the victorious Foreign armies closing in upon them with relentless force.

It was one of those fearful days of heat preceding every rainy season. The Rao Sahib awaited his companions under an awning on the roof of his temporary residence, where any stray breath of wind, however sultry, would be welcome. The sun had not yet risen to dispel the haze that enveloped the surrounding jungle.

The Rani of Jhansi arrived first, quickly followed by Ahmad Khan and other chiefs. Lastly came Tantia Topi with Prasad Singh.

The nobles saluted the Rao Sahib gravely as they appeared upon the roof. Prasad's glance rested for a moment upon the Rani's form, but her gaze was concentrated upon a map of the country. She was apparently not aware of his presence. He took his seat the furthest from her position, after exchanging with Ahmad Khan a formal greeting.

Since his dismissal from Jhansi, Prasad had come to regard the Mohammedan's actions leading up to that event with suspicion. He had formed no definite charge to prefer against Ahmad, but if they should meet again he had determined not to place so much confidence in the other's protestations of friendship. He reasoned that they had not gone far to assist him in the past.

Toward the Rani, who appeared in his eyes more beautiful than before, neither time nor absence had diminished his affection. It was true that while he had come to regard the act for which his banishment had been pronounced as inexcusable; the severe, the unjust criticism upon his private life by one, who, if Ahmad's words were to be given credence, was herself not blameless, for long rankled in his breast.

But had Ahmad Khan spoken the truth concerning her? In the face of the universal praise bestowed upon her virtue and bravery, a doubt had risen in his mind of the Mohammedan's good faith. The doubt grew strong within him during the night ride from Kalpi, and stronger still after the manner in which she fought her way to his rescue at the battle of Kunch. If Ahmad had slandered the Rani's character, had acted as a traitor, he vowed he would slay him without mercy. But in the meantime she had closed his mouth indefinitely. She had laid an interdict upon any expression of his sentiment. He could not speak of these things again until such time as she would grant permission. All he could do was to prove the depth of his love by such actions as her rescue from Jhansi. For the rest, he could only hope that fortune would give him an opportunity to rend the veil of misfortune that had shrouded his life in Jhansi, and appear before her in his true character—a character much tempered by the trials and hardships he had since experienced.

When all were assembled there ensued a period of silence. No one among them seemed to find courage in his heart to speak. Indeed, what was there that could be said? Their fortresses and arsenals had all been captured; their armies vanquished and dispersed; the Foreigners everywhere triumphant. It seemed that only one topic remained for discussion—how to escape the vengeance that would surely fall upon their heads.

The Rani raised her eyes and glanced round upon their despondent countenances. Upon not one of them could she detect a spark of hope remaining. They were as cowed animals awaiting the lash of a master, for offenses which they knew to be unpardonable, in defeat.

"Well, my Lords," she spoke calmly, "I presume that being all gathered, our business is to discuss the next place to give the enemy a battle."

"Give the enemy a battle," Tantia Topi echoed in faint-hearted accents. "What force of men, what guns, what ammunition, do we now possess with which to give battle to the Foreigners. Where even can we fly, to gain any but a temporary refuge"?

"That," returned the Rani firmly, "may be the saving of our situation. We cannot fly, therefore we must fight."

"Fight," echoed Tantia Topi gloomily. "Have we not fought already, and what has been the result? Perhaps the noble Rani," he added, with a strain of sarcasm, "will instruct us how to wage a war without men or guns."

Tantia Topi had not escaped the feeling of jealousy among certain of the leaders, as a result of the praise lavished by the troops upon the personal valor of the Rani of Jhansi.

She retorted with rising temper.

"Ah"! she cried. "Have we not had some experience how fifteen hundred men well-led can give battle to, and defeat over twenty thousand? Now it is our turn to win a victory against overwhelming odds."

"Perhaps the valiant Rani will instruct us further," the Native general suggested, controlling his anger with difficulty, at the Rani's reference to his Jhansi defeat.

The Rao Sahib interposed, fearful of an altercation between his two most skillful commanders.

"Assuredly, fair Lady," he said, "any suggestion for a way to retrieve our disasters will be most welcome."

"Then, my Lords," she continued, as if suggesting a plan that presented little difficulty of accomplishment, "it is simply, that either by strategy, diplomacy, or assault, we do capture Gwalior."

"Gwalior! Gwalior"! passed from mouth to mouth, while looks of incredulous amazement broke upon all faces.

"Gwalior, noble Rani," repeated the Rao Sahib. "Surely thou must mean some other place, not Maharaja Sindhia's impregnable stronghold, garrisoned by twenty thousand Foreign drilled troops."

The Rani rose to her feet and spoke with gathering animation.

"Aye, noble Rao Sahib, I do mean Gwalior, Maharaja Sindhia's capital and no other. I beg your patience," she proceeded, "while I disclose my plan further. With us here, we have, or may gather together on the march, perhaps eight thousand troops—a force with which much may be accomplished, as Tantia Topi knows."

She glanced at the Native hero of numerous defeats with a slight expression of contempt about her lips, and continued:

"Good, then, with these I propose that we make forced marches immediately upon Gwalior, and arrive there before Sindhia has been warned of the coming of his guests. It is well known, my Lords, that Maharaja Sindhia is, at heart, in sympathy with our cause. It is also well known," she added with exquisite naïvete, "that he is a young man not insensible to the charms of a fair woman. To Sindhia, then, I purpose to dispatch a messenger beseeching him to grant me an interview. If he doth grant it, be assured there will be no battle before Gwalior. He will join us with all his forces. But if his crafty minister, Dinkar Rao, or his Foreign councilor, doth persuade him that the Rani of Jhansi's eyes will bewitch his reason to perdition, and he doth refuse my emissary; then we will take his capital whether he be disposed to yield or no. His people are our people; his troops our troops; discreet messengers may induce many to join us at the critical moment, if he elects to give us battle. Gwalior captured," she cried with flashing eyes, "and all Northern India lies at our feet. The Foreigners cannot march upon us immediately, for the rains will make the roads impassable. Thousands will rally to our side. Our swords will again flash across the heavens. Who knows not only Jhansi, but Delhi may be recaptured. Is not this a prize worth staking our frail lives upon? But even if defeat is again the will of God, if die we must; is it not better to perish as warriors should, in a feat of arms upon which the eyes of our enemies will gaze with marvel, than as wild beasts hunted through the jungle?

"Ah, my Lords," she appealed to them with superb emotional fervor. "Let not us cherish despair, but take to our hearts that invincible faith in ourselves, by which the seemingly impossible is often successfully accomplished. Now is the hour when the steel of our courage is forever determined. Let us at least drag from the unwilling tongues of these Foreigners the admission, that the glorious traditions of our race are not to be closed in the pages of history, without reference to a sublime, a mighty funeral."

The Rani's hearers gazed upon her in wonder. That the force of her argument; the fire of her words, swept toward them as a blast from a furnace of heroism, had kindled in their breasts a responsive flame of her own dauntless spirit, was evident: but they were appalled, dumbfounded at the audacity, the daring of her proposal.

To march upon Gwalior in the demoralized condition of their army, in their own sickening despair. Gwalior protected by the strongest fortress in all India, that was regarded, even by Sindhia's Foreign allies as impregnable. Gwalior the capital of the great Maharaja, containing the pick of the Native army and vast stores of munitions of war. No! It could not be done, they agreed mentally. The plan to their minds did not offer the single chance out of a thousand in a forlorn hope.

The Rao Sahib sighed deeply. He gravely shook his head from side to side.

"It is impossible, I fear, brave Rani," he replied. "It would be easier to recapture Delhi, than seize Gwalior from Sindhia's hands."

"Impossible! Impossible"! the others echoed sadly.

Even the fierce nature of Ahmad Khan for once failed to respond to an enterprise of such overpowering odds. But in his mind, the reappearance of his rival, had inflamed his jealousy and hatred to subvert all other feelings. His eyes, at intervals, had glanced suspiciously from the Rani to her lover. Though he had detected no signs of affectionate regard pass from one to the other, he knew that between himself and Prasad, her heart in its entirety, if not her favor, went forth to the noble of her own faith.

Despair, not of an ultimate triumph over the enemy, nor as the result of the blood-stained conscience which certain among the Foreigners asserted she possessed, but despair of her ability to move her companions to one of those splendid achievements of warfare, by which campaigns are turned suddenly in favor of the vanquished, seized upon her spirit. It stimulated all the heroism of her nature to an outburst of feeling. She could no longer withhold the whip of scorn to thrash their courage into action.

"Then stay, my Lords," she cried, "and rest yourselves in Gopalpur. The weather is hot and uncomfortable, for such work as this of Gwalior. But I—I with my Valaitis, even if not another one doth follow, will go to Sindhia's fortress, and either bid defiance to the Foreigners from its walls, or yield my life into the hands of God."

Ahmad's martial spirit was stung by the taunt. He would have risen to his feet in support of the heroic woman, had not a quicker action on Prasad's part restrained him, in sullen humor, to his seat.

The Rani had turned as if about to leave the council, when Prasad crossed over to her side. He drew his sword and laid it at her feet.

"If no other will follow," he cried, "I will go with thee to Gwalior, or to wherever thou dost lead."

The Rani rewarded him with a grateful look, in which he might have discerned the shade of a more tender feeling. She bent down, and taking his sword gave it back to him.

"Thou shalt go with me to Gwalior," she spoke gently.

The Rao Sahib had listened throughout the Rani's appeal with a growing appreciation of its truth. Some great, some telling stroke must be delivered in the emergency. It needed but an incident like Prasad's act to win him over to her side.

"Aye," he exclaimed. "Prasad Singh doth rightly. We will all go with thee, valiant Rani. The command, too, of this business shall be given to thy hands. If Gwalior is captured, the glory of it shall forever rest upon thy head."

The Rani was quick to encourage with praise the turn of opinion in her favor.

"Now do I know, as I had ever believed," she cried joyfully, "that thou art all brave men. Within a week, I vow the Peshwa shall be proclaimed in Sindhia's palace.

"And so," she added, "that we are no longer divided in this matter, I would select the one to go forward as my emissary to Sindhia. Ahmad's valor would entitle him to the dangerous mission, but that, without offense to any present, it would be better to dispatch a Hindu noble as an envoy to a Hindu prince. Otherwise the

Maharaja may regard our aim as too much in the interest of the court of Delhi. Thus I would urge that Prasad Singh doth set forth immediately on this errand, while we close in upon his steps to-night."

"I have said thy will shall be the order of our march, brave Rani," returned the Rao Sahib. "Prasad Singh will go as thy messenger to the Maharaja forthwith."

The Rani turned toward her lover.

"Go then, good Prasad," she enjoined, "and in thy most skillful manner seek to obtain for me an audience with Sindhia, at some place without the walls of Gwalior secure from treachery. Go, and may God's blessing rest upon thy head.

"So, my Lords," she cried. "Let us to Gwalior with cautious speed, and good fortune smiling on our efforts."

The nobles rose spontaneously and shouted with rekindled spirits:

"To Gwalior! To Gwalior"!

The cry was caught up by the soldiers on guard in the compound:

"To Gwalior! To Gwalior! Death to the enemy. Victory for the Rani of Jhansi."

Chapter XXII

VICTORY

FROM remote ages Gwalior had been one of the chief cities of India, owing to the immense natural strength of its position. Many races, succeeding one another, had reared their dwellings about the foot of the huge pile of rock, rising in grim, deep shadowed precipices on all sides, two to three hundred feet from a broken plain, to a plateau crowned by the massive fortress, a mile and a half in length by three hundred yards wide. By a single narrow path alone could the summit be gained.

Numerous had been the splendid palaces, temples, and mausoleums erected in the vicinity by dynasties swept away, and ruins only of the Baradari, once the most superb hall of audience in the world, marks the site of the colossal residence of the Moguls.

In part skirting the suburbs of the city, the Morar river winds northward to its junction with the Chambal, thence its waters reach the Jumna, to mingle finally with those of the holy Ganges. Beyond the Morar, at a considerable distance rocky hills bordering the plain, afford a first line of defense, the few defiles being easily rendered impassable by fortified works.

Such was the place the Rani of Jhansi's daring spirit had determined to seize. It was rich in long accumulated treasure to refill an empty purse, rich in the heirlooms of one of the greatest Native families, and in war material to arm new levies of troops, and thus prolong the strife to an indefinite period. As a prize to fall into her hands, there was scarcely its equal at the moment in India. The moral effect of the successful accomplishment of the act, upon both parties to the struggle, would almost equal that of the capture of Delhi at the commencement of hostilities.

On the morning of the Thirtieth of May, Maharaja Jaiaji Rao Sindhia, the ruling prince of the great Maratha house of Gwalior, had finished his devotions and was about to partake of his usual frugal early meal of milk, bread, and fruit, when a servant delivered a surprising, and, on the whole, an unwelcome piece of news.

An emissary of the Rani of Jhansi had arrived at the palace, and requested an immediate audience with his Highness.

During the year past, Sindhia had heard much of the redoutable Princess of Jhansi. He had been told of her beauty, her wisdom, and her valor. He had followed with sympathetic interest the capable administration of the government of her state, her defense of Jhansi, and latterly, with secret regret, the misfortunes which had descended on her head. So much for his private feeling toward the Rani.

But in public he had followed the advice of his astute minister, Dinkar Rao, who persuaded him to remain an ally of the Foreigners, against his natural impulse to cast in his lot with the Native cause. This, for a sufficient, if not a patriotic reason. While Sindhia bore no love for the Foreigners, he experienced less for the Peshwa as the supreme head of the Marathas, and less still, if not actual hatred, for the ruling Mohammedan family of Delhi.

"If," argued Dinkar Rao, "the Foreigners are driven out of India, who will grasp the great scepter? Surely either the Peshwa or the Emperor of Delhi. What then will become of Maharaja Sindhia? He will be, as of old, a feudatory of an avaricious Native monarch. Better is it to submit to the lesser evil, the comparatively light yoke of the Foreigners."

Maharaja Sindhia perceived the wisdom of his minister's argument, and in spite of the execrations of his troops and people, remained the Foreigners' faithful ally, when his influence cast into the scale on the other side, might have ended their rule in India.

His first thought on hearing of the arrival of the Rani's messenger, was that she was about to look to him for an asylum of refuge. Under the circumstances he devoutly wished she would seek the protection of some other prince. Her presence in Gwalior would surely again stir up his people, many of whom, without his permission, had joined the ranks of the Native army. Then if he were compelled to hand her over to the Foreigners, the act would be so unpopular, that it might be unsafe for him to remain in his own state. He reasoned thus, while he sent in haste for his minister to take advice before consenting to receive the Rani's envoy.

Dinkar Rao was as much perturbed as his master over the intelligence. He hastened to Sindhia, resolved to urge a refusal of the Rani's petition whatever might be its import. He, too, arrived at the hasty conclusion that she was desirous of seeking a refuge in Gwalior. It would, he reasoned with the unscrupulous nature of a born diplomat, have laid the Foreigners under a lasting debt of gratitude, if she could be tricked by fair promises to place herself in Sindhia's power, and then handed over to the mercy of her enemies. But he feared the vengeance of the people, who regarded her as the champion of a righteous cause. At all costs the Rani of Jhansi must be kept away from Gwalior.

These sentiments he strenuously urged upon Sindhia, before it was decided to accord the interview.

Prasad Singh entered Sindhia's presence as became the emissary of a great princess. He saluted the Maharaja with dignified respect, and then proceeded to unfold his mission.

The Rani of Jhansi, he announced, with other illustrious princes and generals, and an army of eight thousand men, were now encamped at Bahadurpur nine miles distant.

Both Sindhia and Dinkar Rao started. This was not the usual way a fugitive sought protection. They at once perceived a greater peril in the situation than they had imagined. Not that they feared for Gwalior itself as a fortress, but concerning the people. Could they depend upon the fidelity of their troops in such an emergency?

Against any other leader, probably; but the name of the Rani of Jhansi made it more than doubtful. In the temples prayers were constantly rising for her safety.

Sindhia replied to the envoy, by asking the purpose of the Rani of Jhansi at the head of so large a force within his territory.

"Her Highness," Prasad returned evasively, "is but marching from Gopalpur to the north, and has halted to pay her respects to the great Maharaja of Gwalior. She is desirous of a personal interview with a prince of whom she has heard so many words of praise."

Sindhia's feelings were stirred conflictingly. He would have sacrificed much personally to behold the woman, of whom all men spoke in such enthusiastic terms. He would have been glad to receive her with the highest honors; but the shadows of the Peshwa, the Emperor, and the Foreigners haunted his mind.

"Doth the Rani then desire to enter Gwalior"? he asked anxiously.

"Such, my Lord Sindhia," Prasad replied, "is far from her Highness's present intention. She trusts to meet the great ruler of Gwalior merely in friendly intercourse at some point without the city. To this end only do my instructions extend."

Sindhia found himself in a dilemma. To refuse this apparently simple request might seem an ungracious act. Besides, he was anxious to judge of the beauty and charm of which others raved continually. Surely there could be little harm in extending to her this outward mark of his respect. If the Foreigners blamed him subsequently, he could plead the danger of the situation. He might even assert that his object was to urge upon her to surrender.

But Dinkar Rao was of a different mind. His master's *zanana,* tenanted by more than one beauty, was a conspicuous proof of the youthful Maharaja's susceptibility to the charms of fair women. Whatever covert object the Rani might have in view, and from her character he suspected an ulterior design cloaked by the harmless nature of her request, he feared that Sindhia would be carried away by her smile if not by her force of argument. So he took upon himself to reply by a pointed question.

"Thus far, well, my Lord Prasad Singh, but the Maharaja Sindhia should be informed first, how it comes about that the Rani of Jhansi prefers her request with an armed force so near to Gwalior, instead of sending forth her envoy from the boundary of the state, asking permission to approach the capital. To my mind it does not display great respect on her part for the authority of Maharaja Sindhia."

The concluding statement was directed as much to the sensibility of his master as it was by way of reply to the Rani's envoy. It had the designed effect. Sindhia's pride was nettled.

"Aye," he acquiesced. "My minister speaks wisely. Doth the Rani of Jhansi suppose my territory is to be invaded at the will of any neighboring ruler? That question must be answered to our satisfaction."

"My Lord Maharaja," Prasad replied. "I have no doubt the Rani will, herself, make her action excusable to your Highness. We live in times of strife when the customs of peace are swept aside out of necessity. Your Highness, as a great Indian prince, will surely not view with disfavor the Rani's conduct in defending her rights against the Foreigners."

The appeal touched Sindhia's heart. Before his mind rose the image of the valiant Princess, fighting for her throne, their united country and religion. He hesitated to return an answer. It was a critical moment for the fortunes of his house.

Dinkar Rao quickly perceived the effect of the sympathetic chord touched by the envoy He seized the opportunity to impress upon his master's ears a discordant note.

"Of the misfortunes of the Rani of Jhansi," he said, "Maharaja Sindhia cannot be unmindful, but," he added with significance, "among her allies are representatives of the Peshwa and the Emperor. These are no friends of Sindhia. Rather are they more his enemies than the Foreigners. It is my advice that the Maharaja does not meet the Rani with these people. It is my advice that he doth require the Rani to immediately withdraw from his dominions."

"Aye, thou speakest well, Dinkar Rao," remarked

Sindhia. "The Rao Sahib has no right to come with armed men into my territory."

Prasad was not prepared for this trend of argument. He again besought Sindhia to grant the Rani her request; but Dinkar Rao's policy prevailed. Sindhia would not receive her in such company as that of the Rao Sahib and Ahmad Khan. She must retreat beyond his borders forthwith, or abide the consequences. Such was his ultimate decision. He was probably glad to be afforded so plausible an excuse for refusing hospitality to the Foreigners' enemy.

Thus Prasad was reluctantly obliged to return to the Rȧni's camp with the information that his mission had failed.

"So Dinkar Rao," the Rani cried, "is fearful that I might win his master to our cause. We will then take his capital."

On the First of June the sun rose to discover the armies of the Rani of Jhansi and Maharaja Sindhia confronting each other on the plain of Gwalior. In the distance the great rock with its fortifications stood out defiantly against the sky.

Overnight, Sindhia had been informed that the Rani's forces, so far from obeying his injunction to retire from his state, were advancing upon the city. It left him no alternative but to give battle.

Sindhia had occupied a strategic position on rising ground, his flanks protected by squadrons of cavalry, his center formed by artillery. A splendid body of six hun-

Her horse leaped forward, straight for Sindhia's guns.—Page 255.

dred nobles and retainers guarded the person of the Maharaja.

Across the plain, the Rani had thrown out a light screening force of skirmishers. Behind these she had placed herself at the head of her Valaitis, with Prasad bearing her standard once more proudly aloft. Again in rear was her artillery and infantry, with the remainder of her cavalry under Ahmad Khan in reserve, either to support her in case of need, or to dash for Gwalior the moment the day was won.

The Rani wore on her head a Persian cap of steel, richly ornamented with figures of beaten gold, a spike of the same precious metal, and feathery aigrettes. Her hands and wrists were protected by gauntlets of metal scale work. It was evident she did not intend to direct the battle from a spot secure from the danger of shot or blows. Every inch did she appear as one of those intrepid Maratha warriors, who had defied the power of the great Mogul, in order to carve kingdoms and principalities for themselves out of his empire.

Presently Sindhia's guns opened on the advancing foe. They swept the open space between the two armies with devastating force, driving the Rani's skirmishers back upon the main body. For a few minutes the smoke hid the two forces from each other. It was the moment the Rani looked for to deliver a telling blow.

She turned in her saddle and raised her sword. A bugle rang out the clear notes of the charge. Her horse leaped forward straight for Sindhia's guns, with her troopers thundering in her wake. Onward she dashed heedless, and unharmed by the shot and shell, up to the wall of smoke, and through it to the belches of cannon flame. With a terrific yell her troopers came upon the gunners, driving them from their posts. Sindhia's first line broke and fled. The Rani had captured his guns.

Sindhia's glance swept over the field in alarm. He had ordered his infantry to support the artillery and they had refused to obey. If his ears did not deceive him, they were shouting the Rani of Jhansi's name. A decisive moment had come. Something must be done or the battle was lost. He ordered his bodyguard to charge before the Rani's troopers could reform or she could receive support.

The Rani accepted the challenge, rallied her troopers as best she could, and boldly fronted the oncoming force. The shock was terrific, the ensuing *mêlée* of cursing, shouting, fighting horsemen, desperate. In the heart of it all the Rani's sword flashed above her head, delivering sweeping blows. Wherever her standard, slashed and pierced with sabre cuts and bullets, waved, there the fight seemed hottest. Her life appeared to be shielded by a charm. At one time she had cut her way near to Sindhia's person.

"Sindhia! Sindhia"! she cried. "Art thou as much afraid of the Rani's sword as thou art of her eyes. Stay but a moment, as I would exchange a few strokes with thee."

But Sindhia had seen enough of the day. The ferocious Valaitis were routing his bodyguard, his infantry had gone over to the enemy, the Rani's main force was advancing to cut off his retreat. In the distance he beheld the enemy's reserve cavalry sweeping across the plain to seize his capital. With a few horsemen, he turned and galloped from the field to his Foreign allies at Agra.

A great victory had at last crowned the Rani's arms, the battle of Bahadurpur was won; she had kept her promise, Gwalior lay at her feet.

Chapter XXIII

HAIL! PRINCESS of the MARATHAS

WELL might the Native leaders give themselves over to a transport of exultation. The victory had been so complete, Sindhia's flight so hasty, that not a rupee of vast treasure, not a gem of the hoard of a century, had been saved from their hands. Within an hour they found their condition changed from being little better than that of a routed mob, to the possessors of an impregnable stronghold, a splendid armament of modern guns, a new force of ten thousand well drilled troops, stores and munitions of war in abundance. More than this the people of Gwalior received them, not as conquerors, but as champions of their race.

Early in the afternoon the Rani of Jhansi rode into Gwalior on the right hand of the Rao Sahib. Thousands of people came forth to meet her, shouting her name in a frenzy of joy. As she approached the gates, a salute of artillery burst from the fortress, high above their heads. She gazed upward to behold her banner replacing Sindhia's on the loftiest pinnacle. It was the result of Prasad's first order, on taking possession of the fortress in the name of the Rani of Jhansi, as well as that of the Rao Sahib.

On the steps of the palace they were received by a group of liberated Maratha nobles, who had been imprisoned by Sindhia to please his Foreign allies. Their patriotism had so dominated their discretion that the last few months had been passed within the walls of the Gwalior fortress. They greeted their deliverers with effusions of welcome.

In Sindhia's palace confusion reigned. The chief ladies of the *zanana,* his wives and concubines, had heard from time to time of the exploits of the Rani of Jhansi, certainly with astonishment. But in the privacy of his family life, Sindhia had not been so fearful of expressing his admiration for the heroic woman. Consequently she found little favor in the minds of the voluptuous companions of his leisure hours. In the atmosphere of gossip and jealousy in which they existed, they were inclined to regard her as a bold creature of less than doubtful virtue, otherwise she could not consort so openly with men. Unlike the poor and humble of their sex, who beheld in her an incarnation of the glorious Uma, the Goddess of Light and all things beautiful, they ascribed her power to the influence of the sinister Durga, under whose protection they charitably asserted she was preserved from death. Thus she grew in their eyes to be a terrible, awe-inspiring figure, and they fled from Gwalior faster than their noble lord, the Maharaja, on the first news that she was about to enter the city——, white bundles of humanity, riding for life across the plain, with Ahmad Khan in vain pursuit. He was loath to be deprived of the fairest spoil of victory.

It was shortly decided that Sindhia's personal treasure

was to be divided equally among the Native leaders, all the jewels, silks, and robes found in the *zanana* to become the property of the Rani of Jhansi as by natural right. From the state treasury a bountiful supply of largess was to be drawn to recompense both their own troops and those of Sindhia, who had joined them at the critical moment. A grand *Darbar* was summoned by the Rao Sahib to meet that evening in the great hall of Sindhia's palace, to proclaim the Peshwa supreme Lord of the Marathas, and to reward the leaders for their loyalty to the cause.

In the enthusiasm of the hour, all signs of past misfortunes, or of those which might yet descend, were swept from the exultant countenances of nobles and officers, congratulating each other upon the prize that had been won.

When darkness had fallen, the *Darbar* hall presented a scene of unsurpassed magnificence. From huge crystal chandeliers suspended from the roof, hundreds of candles illuminated the ornately carved pillars and capitals, the inlaid pavement, the walls, a blaze of light in the reflections of silver-framed mirrors. On either side of the throne gilded chairs of state had been placed, but it was upon the contents of sundry gold dishes, that the eyes of the gathering throng feasted.

They were piled high with ornaments scintillating sparks of colored fire from Sindhia's hoard of emeralds, rubies, diamonds, and sapphires.

Upon one tray reposed a single jeweled casket, evidently containing some priceless trinket. Several argued with each other over the question for whom it was destined as a reward.

Presently, the Rao Sahib entered the hall from a door near the throne. Toward the figure of the Rani of Jhansi at his side the attention of all was immediately drawn. Against her desire to appear in her uniform, she had been persuaded to attire herself in the state robes of the senior Rani of Gwalior, silks of many hues, stiff with pearl embroidery. A splendid crown of rubies and diamonds rose above her forehead, her girdle was heavy with precious stones.

The Rao Sahib conducted her to a seat immediately on the right of the throne, when as the Peshwa's representative he took a standing position directly in front of the vacant chair of royal authority. Behind them, and on either side, the nobles in their train grouped themselves effectively.

As they looked from the dais they beheld the great hall filled to its utmost capacity with eager upturned faces. Curtains screening the apertures had been withdrawn, disclosing crowded ante-chambers and passages. Could their gaze have penetrated further they would have seen a vast concourse surging about the entrance to the palace and in the courtyard beyond. These did not so much await the proclamation as another common object in mind.

The Rao Sahib moved to the edge of the dais, and read a brief declaration of the Peshwa's titles.

It was received with applause, though it was apparent their enthusiasm was restrained.

He then proceeded to distribute favors. Upon the shoulders of the nobles recently imprisoned for their sympathy with the Native cause, he placed robes of honor. To others were given important offices and commands.

The recipients were each cheered loudly, but soon looks of mute inquiry broke on many faces.

Was there then to be no reward for her who had won all this glory for their arms?

Thus, while Sindhia's jewels were being divided, in the background, several grew impatient. They began to call upon the Rani's name.

"Shame! Shame"! they murmured. "Is it not the Rani of Jhansi who should receive honor above all others"?

One taller than the rest silenced the complaint for the moment.

"The casket," said he, "yet remains. Hush! Perchance it contains the greatest treasure for the Queen."

The jewels were at last disposed of to the satisfaction of some and the disappointment of others. The Rao Sahib turned, and took the Rani lightly by the hand. He led her before the throne.

Then was it that the enthusiasm of every heart burst forth in a mighty cheer, that shook Sindhia's palace to its foundations. In the halls, courts, and corridors, it was tumultuously echoed; the throng without caught it up, and hurled it above the city to the black walls of the fortress, where a woman's banner was fluttering in a gentle current of air.

They knew their valiant Queen was about to receive her reward.

It was long impossible for the Rao Sahib to obtain a hearing. The Rani seemed to shrink from the storm of affectionate regard her rising had called forth. She realized that she had won a greater victory than Gwalior, the laurels of which no enemy could snatch from her brow. She had captured the hearts of the people.

Again and again the Rao Sahib endeavored to enjoin silence, but it was temporarily obtained in one part only to be lost afresh in half a dozen quarters. At last he addressed those nearest to the dais.

"My Lord Rajas," said he, "I need not present to you the great Lady who stands before the throne. To the noble Rani of Jhansi belongs all praise for the glory of this day. As imperishable as the fortress rock of Gwalior, her name will stand forth in the history of our race. By the will of the most illustrious Peshwa, I give to her the supreme command of the army of Gwalior, and for her adornment Sindhia's most cherished jewels. For the rest, is she not yours, to honor as you please"?

Prasad had left his place in the suite, and taken the casket in his hands. He raised the lid and approached the Rani. Silence fell upon the expectant throng.

With care he took from the casket rope after rope of matchless pearls. It was Sindhia's state necklace, once of the Imperial Regalia of Portugal.

He handed the casket to another, and then gently hung the treasure about the Rani's neck.

Swiftly he stepped back a pace or two. His sword flashed in mid-air as his voice resounded throughout the hall.

"Hail! Lachmi Bai, Rani of Jhansi. Hail! Victor of Gwalior, Princess of the Marathas."

His voice died away for a moment without response, then the storm of enthusiasm burst forth anew. It grew into a frenzy almost approaching madness. They shouted that she should be proclaimed Queen of Gwalior as well as Jhansi. The Rao Sahib became apprehensive that she might be swept on the wave of popular favor even to the dignity of the Peshwa's throne.

Without, the plaudits increased above the tumult in the hall. An officer with difficulty elbowed his way to the dais. He delivered a message to the Rao Sahib.

"The people," he cried, "would have the Rani of Jhansi come forth so that they may behold the light of her countenance."

The Rao Sahib glanced uneasily over the surging mass and protested.

"I fear for her person," he said. Then he asked. "Can they not be appeased in some other way? If thou wert to scatter money among them."

"Noble Rao Sahib," the officer replied. "A hail of gold *mohrs* would not satisfy their humor. They will see the great Rani, the Victor of Gwalior."

"Aye, my Lord," the Rani interposed. "Surely will

I go to the steps of the palace. These poor people. Do I not love them? If it pleases them to see but a frail being like themselves, their desire is easily gratified."

She took the crown from her head and gave it to an attendant, replacing it with the folds of a shawl. Then she moved down amid the cheering soldiers thronging the hall and passages to the steps of the portico. There a vast multitude confronted her eyes. Torches flared upward to illumine exultant faces. Their plaudits were redoubled as they beheld her come forth attended by the other leaders of the cause. She moved a few paces in front of the pillars rising on either side, and stood gazing wistfully, wonderingly upon the scene. It was to her, and to her alone, that their admiration, their love went forth in a whirlwind of vociferous applause; but she failed to grasp its entire significance. She could have demanded the Peshwa's crown, and they would have set it on her head. She received the tribute only as a vindication of her actions in upholding her rights with the sword.

It was her hour of triumph.

The scene was less to the liking of the Rao Sahib even than that within the palace. The Rani of Jhansi had clearly become the fountain of honor and authority with the people. Had he understood her nature better he need not have harbored fear.

Presently those nearest to the portico would have it that they could gaze upon her face more clearly.

Obediently she threw back the folds of her shawl, disclosing all her features to their view—strength, determination, heroism, displayed in their classic outlines.

"Ah, dear Rani," a trooper cried. "Beautiful Queen of Jhansi. Behold how the people do love thee."

The words smote her heart, causing a spring of emotion to burst forth. On the instant she became the woman in place of the redoutable warrior. She turned as if seeking a place of retreat to hide her feelings.

Prasad in waiting near by, noticed her appeal, and strode to her side.

The Defender of Jhansi, the Victor of Gwalior, raised her hands to her face, laid her head on his shoulder, and wept.

Prasad gently led the Rani from the scene. He conducted her through a silent corridor to a door that opened into the palace gardens. Thence to a pavilion set apart for the use of the ladies of Sindhia's *zanana.* The noise and uproar died away, the stillness of night fell upon them, for long neither spoke.

At last the Rani broke the trend of a deep reverie.

"Prasad," she asked. "Art thou not going to the banquet? See, there are lights yonder in the windows of the great hall. Thou wilt miss the feast in honor of our victory."

"What care I for feasts, dear Lady," he returned, "so that I may stay with thee."

"Thou art changed then, Prasad"? she replied.

"How dost thou mean"? he questioned. "Changed in some manner I pray God I am; but never was there a

"Never have I hungered for aught else but thee, fair Rani."—Page 267.

time since I first set eyes upon thy graceful form, when I hungered for aught else, but thee, fair Rani."

"Ah! Prasad, surely thy memory is at fault," she retorted. "I no longer blame thee for it, if truly thou art changed, but there was a time when thou didst prefer to drink of Foreign spirits, and enjoy the charms of *natch* girls, rather than obey the summons of the Rani."

"Never," he cried vehemently. "I vow it is not so. Explain more of this I do beseech thee, so that I may perceive clearly the source of the untruth."

"I would not recall the matter, only to satisfy thee," she answered, "but when thou wert a guest of Ahmad Khan, dost not remember his enthralling dancer? Ah! fickle one," she rebuked him lightly. "Has Ganga's face, too, vanished from thy mind"?

"In truth," Prasad affirmed. "Her face never was in my mind to vanish from it. With thy dear face ever before my eyes, I beheld no other, not even as a passing fancy."

"Say you so"? she spoke quickly. "Yet Ahmad Khan vowed most reluctantly that thou wert so drunk with wine, so intoxicated with thy passion for the girl, that thou couldst not be brought to listen to my voice."

Prasad started, as the late suspicion of his friend's treachery began to receive confirmation.

"Tell me! Tell me"! he urged. "Did he convey my message to thee, that I was sick, that I yearned for a glance from thine eyes to heal my malady"?

"Truly he did not," the Rani answered. "No such message did he ever bring."

Prasad sprang to his feet impulsively.

"The lying, treacherous Moslem," he ejaculated fiercely. "Farewell for a little space, great Rani. For this he shall answer even at the banquet. I will slay him in his seat."

"Nay, stay, good Prasad," she enjoined.

"Aye, but thou dost not know all," he returned vehemently.

"But I would know all," she answered calmly, "before thou dost commit so rash an act."

"Dear Rani! Ah God, that there could be such vileness coiled like a serpent round any creature's heart. What wouldst thy order be, if I were to disclose to thee, that yonder villain, had sworn thy ears were too full of the love words of another Moslem to hear of my petition, that his name so hung upon thy lips as to stifle any message in return, thine eyes so captivated with his form that thou hadst yielded thy virtue to his passion as readily as a lotus bending its fair head before a storm? Such was thy case with Dost Ali; he swore upon his cursed Koran, and so he stirred my nature until I lost my reason. What now, great Rani, is thy pleasure, thy command"?

He waited, breathing heavily with emotion, for the order he anticipated would burst forth from the outraged woman's lips to exterminate the Mohammedan. But it did not come.

For a moment, and for a moment only, she was

tempted thus to act. An angry glance swept to the lighted windows of the banquet hall. But she perceived the fatal consequences of a blood feud stirred up at that feast. It might be ruinous to the brightening prospects of the cause she cherished more than all else.

"Prasad," she replied deliberately. "It is a lie. We have both been wronged. But as God this day has answered my prayers, I doubt not he will judge between us and Ahmad."

"What! Shall I not then go hence and slay him"? Prasad demanded.

"Nay," she replied restrainingly. "Hast thou forgotten how we stood in Jhansi? So do we stand here in Gwalior. All is not yet gained. Be assured the Foreigners will return. We need Ahmad's sword, more than his dead body in revenge. Ah! my dear Lord," she exclaimed with rapture, "Let us forget his wickedness in this hour of joy—in this hour of our reconciliation," she added in a lower tone.

He knelt at her side, then took her yielding form in his arms. He drew her closer and closer to his breast.

"Prasad! Prasad! I do love thee," she whispered softly.

"To the end, dear one, to the end," he passionately returned.

From the banquet hall the sounds of high revelry came across the garden borne upon air laden with the perfume of flowers; but, in time, the lights were extinguished, and only the watchwords of the sentries on the citadel fell upon their ears. The veil of darkness hid their long embrace, until the bugles of the morn rang out the call to arms.

An hour of triumph and an hour of happiness was past; an hour greater than both was yet to come.

Chapter XXIV

AHMAD'S LAST STRATAGEM

FROM the moment of Prasad's reappearance at Gopalpur Ahmad's jealousy was rekindled to greater force even than in Jhansi. He hated the Hindu noble with all the vindictiveness of his nature. Had stirring events not followed each other with such rapidity, he would have sought a pretext for an open quarrel, and once for all settled their rival claims to the Rani's affection. If he was chagrined at Prasad's selection to act as her envoy to the Maharaja Sindhia, the feeling was intensified on the other being chosen as her standard bearer at Bahadurpur, and by Prasad's telling stroke for her favor in saluting her as Princess of the Marathas at the grand *Darbar*.

At the subsequent banquet he sat in sullen, gloomy humor. He neither spoke nor feasted. At the call to drink of spirits and join in the carousal of the assembled nobles, he pleaded his religious principles as an excuse to withhold his lips from intoxicating liquors.

That the Rani was not present at the banquet was to be expected, but he marked Prasad's absence, and drew conclusions from a guilty conscience. They were together, he surmised. His duplicity was probably discovered. "What then"? he again and again asked himself.

For the vengeance of Prasad he did not fear. His arm was as strong as that of his rival. But he dreaded the form of retribution usually visited at Native courts by a powerful enraged woman. He conjectured that the Rani's resentment would not be displayed in a burst of anger, a dagger thrust openly at his breast; but in one of those covert ways, by which such offenders as himself were disposed of, to terrorize the stoutest heart. He might be invited to an entertainment that led to the dungeon of a fortress, there to die of cholera, so it would be affirmed. Obnoxious people often disappeared without an explanation. The blank of that unknown was fraught with the suggestion of torture, and a lingering death by slow poison.

As Ahmad glanced uneasily round the hall, every shadow seemed to warn him of impending danger. The palace was no safe place for him if the Rani and Prasad were together. He had better, indeed, gain the outside of the walls of Gwalior until he had made up his mind what course to adopt. He rose to carry this idea into immediate effect.

"What, art thou going"? his neighbor asked in a tone of friendly rebuke. "Thou, who art ever the first in war and the last to leave a banquet."

"To-morrow is a fast," Ahmad tersely rejoined. "I would be early at my devotions."

His neighbor laughed banteringly.

"Your devotions"! he exclaimed. "Ah, to be sure,

and to a fair deity, I doubt not. It is ever the way with you Mohammedans. Your Prophet takes good care that his followers are provided with *houris* on earth as well as in heaven. But good luck to you. May she speedily reward your prayers."

"The fool," muttered Ahmad, as he passed from the hall by the nearest exit. "A very yielding deity is the one I have in mind."

With caution he made his way through dark passages and courts out from the palace. He strode rapidly into the narrow, squalid bazaars of Gwalior, directing his steps toward one of the city gates, heedless of the rejoicings of the people among whom he passed. He breathed the night air more freely when he had left the walls behind.

At the camp, which was his first destination, he found the soldiers drinking in celebration of the victory, and disposed to be quarrelsome. He approached his own quarters and sternly ordered a few men, upon whose temporary fidelity he could depend, to saddle their horses. Curses and blows soon brought them to their senses and obedience. In his tent, Ahmad quickly sorted and placed in security about his person, the lighter and more valuable of Sindhia's jewels that had fallen to his share. Then he came forth, mounted his horse, and led the way to a dwelling situated a few miles out from the city.

It was a house he had visited on a previous residence in Gwalior, secluded, and within easy reach of the hills in case of the necessity of flight. It was owned by a member of his religion, who received him with every outward sign of friendship.

There, he determined to remain for a day or two, and by means of spies watch the actions of the Rani and Prasad.

Such news as he did thus receive inflamed his jealousy still further, and confirmed the surmise of danger in his position.

The Rani, it appeared, had taken up her abode in the camp, to direct the maneuvering of troops and the erection of fortifications in the defiles of the hills against a possible return of the enemy. Prasad was observed constantly at her side. It was evident he had entirely regained her favor; it was almost certain the moving hand of the Jhansi intrigue had been detected.

Clearly, to Ahmad's mind, Gwalior was no safe place in which to remain. He had better away before the Rani's vengeance fell.

He argued further, that, for other reasons, a severance of his connection with the Native cause would now be a wise course. The jewels he had obtained from Sindhia's treasure were of considerable value. He had taken other booty, too, that could be turned into ready money through the agency of his Moslem host. With this, he might return to Afghanistan and placate the Amir, from whose anger he had fled, consequent upon the death of a relative of that monarch, charged to Ahmad's long account of such affairs. Besides, what business had he to fight in the Peshwa's name? Had the Emperor of Delhi been proclaimed at the *Darbar,* religious principles might have enjoined upon him the duty of remaining in the field, but he owed no allegiance to the Hindu king. As a fanatic, at heart, he detested the Hindu faith and its followers. His object had been to fight with them, first to vanquish the Foreigners, and then, in the name of the Mogul Emperor, subdue his allies. But that hour was now unlikely ever to come. The Emperor was a prisoner in the Foreigners' hands, and such power as was regained to the Native cause through the victory of the Rani of Jhansi, lay with the Peshwa. He despised and hated the Peshwa, so he decided to withdraw from Gwalior, though not alone. He purposed to carry the Rani with him by force, if such an act were possible. He thought out his plan deeply, for in it there was no little danger.

That night, he determined to ride into the camp and direct one of his followers to seize her from her tent, then away before an alarm could be given or a rescue effected. It was a bold project, but he was prepared to risk much in a last attempt to secure her embrace. If frustrated in the act, he could lie, fight, or fly as circumstances dictated. The chief difficulty lay in discovering her sleeping place, as it was reported she changed her tent nightly. Over this, he pondered, at length arriving at the decision to decoy the Rani's secretary to his house, and by threats compel him to disclose the secret, if it were preserved as such. He sent forth two of his men, discreet in such affairs, to lay hold of Bipin Dat.

As it happened this proved to be an easy matter.

Like the majority of the Rani's followers, Bipin had plunged into a demonstrative celebration of good fortune. With head held aloft and chest expanded, as he considered was the proper carriage for one who stood so near to the person of the Heroine of Gwalior, he had gone forth on the morrow of the victory to impress upon everyone he met the exalted nature of his office. He was thus received by all with protestations of friendship, given the best to eat, and unluckily more spirits to drink than it was prudent for him to imbibe. Alas! For two days the worthy secretary had been absent from his duties.

In sober intervals, marvelous were the stories he recounted of personal valor in battles fought side by side with his great mistress. His audiences gazed upon him with eyes wide open, as they listened with ears of deep attention. At the conclusion of each narrative the brave secretary must accept another cup of spirits. Of a truth the brave secretary seemed as great a drinker as he was a fighter. He always protested, but drank the spirits nevertheless. At last he stumbled across an accursed unbeliever in his prowess, one of those unpleasant people to be found among all nations, who will persist in placing a vocal mark of interrogation after every man's statement.

"At Bahadurpur," Bipin asserted, "six of the Foreigners I killed with this arm. Their Maharaja I would have captured, but that he plunged with his elephant into the jungle."

"How could that be"? asked the incredulous one, "since there were no Foreigners at Bahadurpur, their general does not ride on an elephant, and there is no jungle within leagues of the place. To be sure what thou sayest is doubtless true, honorable sir," he added apologetically, "but other accounts of the battle differ so much; and what am I, but a seeker after the exact truth"?

Bipin glared angrily upon the venturesome man, but his ideas were not in such order, just at the moment, to discover an answer on the tip of his tongue. Fortunately, two men who had sat attentively in a corner came to the relief of his confusion.

"Thou art a miserable fellow," interposed one, addressing the doubter. "If the great secretary says he killed six of the Foreigners at Bahadurpur, they must have been there to be slain. If he asserts the Foreign general escaped on an elephant, did he not possess eyes to note the difference between that beast and a camel. Wert thou at the battle"? he asked pointedly.

"Aye, wert thou at the battle"? echoed the companion, "otherwise thou art an ass to talk in such fashion."

The doubter was compelled to admit that he had not been within miles of the fight, when the secretary's confusion was transferred to his countenance.

Bipin effusively thanked his champions for their belief

in his words. In turn they insisted upon drinking a cup of spirits with so great a man.

"Ah"! exclaimed the first who had spoken, "what would not my poor master give to hear such tales as flow from thy lips."

"Who is thy master"? asked Bipin, with a solemn period between each word.

"The Raja Krishna Singh, great sir," the other replied respectfully, "a Gwalior noble whose infirmities have for long held him to his couch, and prevented his attendance even at the grand *Darbar*. He would receive thee with all honor as the Rani's secretary, and reward thee handsomely if thou wouldst deign to tell all thou knowest of the glorious Queen of Jhansi. Her name is ever in his mind. My companion and myself would gladly lead the way to his house."

Bipin's pride was immensely flattered. His society was now being sought by a raja. Soon he would be a raja himself. With condescension he agreed to accept the invitation, after he had drank another cup of spirits to steady his feet.

"Is it far to thy master's house"? he asked.

"But a short distance beyond the walls, noble Secretary," his new friend replied.

"*Wah!* Then I will go with thee now," Bipin assented.

He endeavored to rise, but the additional cup of spirits had an effect contrary to what was intended. His limbs collapsed under him as if disjointed. He would have been obliged to remain on the spot but for his friends' assistance. They helped him to his feet and out into the bazaar, then with strong arms supporting him on either side, they hurried him to the gate.

For a time, Bipin chattered incoherently about battles, rajas, and palaces; when it began to dawn upon his obscure understanding that he was travelling a great distance. His feet dragged over the road as if weights of iron were chained to his ankles. He begged to be permitted to lie down and sleep. To his dismay his companions gruffly ordered him to move faster. It suddenly occurred to him that he might have been abducted by thieves.

He cried once for help, but a hand promptly laid over his mouth stifled the sound. In a firm grasp he was thrust unwillingly forward.

At last they came to the house occupied by Ahmad Khan, when Bipin was conducted out of the darkness immediately into the Mohammedan's presence.

For a moment the secretary stood blinking in the light with no idea of his surroundings. He had entirely forgotten the object with which he had been induced to set forth from the city; but Ahmad's countenance seemed familiar. Through a mental haze, the thought came to him that one of his uncles had heard of his good fortune, and had arrived to obtain a share of his money. This was a displeasing, if not an entirely unlooked for event, so he determined to disavow the relationship before the other had time to make himself known.

" Go away," he ejaculated, with his eyes fixed stupidly upon Ahmad. " Go away. Thou art a rogue, a lying *fakir.* I swear thou art no uncle of mine."

" What, thou drunken fool," shouted Ahmad in a voice of thunder. " I would as soon be uncle to a litter of swine."

He clutched Bipin by the throat, and held him until the secretary's eyes and tongue protruded. Ahmad hurled him into a corner.

" Get water," he cried, " and throw over the idiot. Then, perhaps he will come to his senses."

But Bipin had arrived at a realization of his position. He recognized Ahmad, and begged forgiveness for his mistake.

" To be sure," he returned feebly. " Thou art my good friend, Ahmad Khan, though a little rough and quick in resenting an error of sight on coming in out of the darkness. I beseech thee to say no more about the pitcher of water."

" That wilt depend how quickly thou canst gather thy wits," Ahmad sternly replied.

" Surely every one of them are now in my head," answered Bipin, frightened at Ahmad's manner. While he endeavored to recollect how it was he had been induced to come to the place, he began to change his previous good opinion of the Mohammedan.

" Then listen," enjoined Ahmad, and speak truly or a

torch applied to thy feet may quicken thy understanding. Dost know in which tent the Rani sleeps to-night"?

As Bipin had not been to the camp, he was not possessed of the information, but under the circumstances he thought it best to withhold his ignorance. In any case, he reasoned, it was probable Ahmad would not place credence on his denial, and might carry his threat of the torch into effect.

"Certainly, great sir," he replied. "If it be thy desire, I am ready to point out the Rani's tent."

"Where is it situated"? Ahmad asked.

This was a difficult question for Bipin to answer offhand. He hesitated a moment before he replied.

"Where is her tent placed"? Ahmad again demanded.

"Great Lord," stammered Bipin, "near to,—I mean on the right of that occupied by her Valaiti guard."

"Thou art assured of this"?

"Noble sir, why should I tell a lie"? Bipin questioned in return.

"Good, then," Ahmad resumed, bending a stern look on the secretary. "In two hours we set forth from the camp. When we arrive there, thou wilt point out the Rani's tent to one of my men. If thou hast spoken the truth, then thou canst go to the devil for aught I care; but if a lie, the Rani will herself have thee well beaten. It is her order that thou dost obey me in this," he added, in response to a surprised look on the secretary's face, "as she awaits a secret message that must fall into no other hands."

Ahmad then withdrew to call down, as usual, the blessing of God on his evil intent; leaving Bipin in charge of an attendant.

An attempt on the secretary's part to discover Ahmad's object further, was met by a silent repulse.

Truly, the situation was not one to afford the secretary cheerful reflections. He knew no more than Ahmad of the position of the Rani's tent, but he trusted that in the scuffle likely to ensue, from an entry into a tent presumed to be that of the Rani, he could escape. He had told a lie in the first place, and was now afraid to disclose the truth. Whatever was the result, he vowed henceforth to transfer his watchful eye from Prasad to Ahmad, as it was evident the Mohammedan had a disagreeable, an unfriendly side to his nature.

" What a miserable existence is this," concluded Bipin. " We have no sooner climbed to a great height, than a rock slips from under our feet, and behold! we are again where we started. If I only get well out of this, no prospect shall tempt me to remain away from my family."

Presently the effect of the secretary's libations overcame his fears, and snores proclaimed unconsciousness.

Bipin had slept for about two hours, when he was awakened by a rough hand laid on his shoulder, while a voice commanded him to rise immediately.

He was led to the outer door of the house, where a group of horsemen, with Ahmad in their midst, were accoutred apparently for a long march. With considerable effort, emphasized by impatient oaths from Ahmad, the secretary was assisted on to the back of a spare charger. Ahmad gave an order, and the party set off at a brisk pace through the darkness of midnight toward the camp—silent, grim visaged figures, ready for any desperate act.

Ahmad approached the camp at a point where he was well known and would be permitted to pass unquestioned. He inquired his way to the headquarters and rode thither with caution. Then he ordered two of his followers to dismount and carry out his previous directions.

There were no lights, and for a space Bipin stumbled about among the tent ropes.

"Thou fool," muttered one of the men. "If thou dost make such a disturbance the whole camp will be awakened. Where is the tent? Point it out quickly and let us get the work over, or the master will slit thy windpipe."

Bipin had not the faintest idea of the Rani's sleeping place, but he indicated a tent at random.

"Siva protect me," he faltered. "What now will happen"?

One of the men approached the tent noiselessly and untied the fastenings. He listened for a moment, when being satisfied apparently that its occupant was still asleep, entered. His companion watched outside.

In a minute the man reappeared bearing a struggling woman's form in his arms, with one hand over her mouth to prevent an outcry. He hurried to the waiting troop and relinquished his burden to Ahmad. The two men then vaulted on to their horses, and the whole party were off without a cry, or a word exchanged.

Bipin remained for some moments a prey to fear and astonishment. Then it broke upon his mind that he had betrayed his mistress for some evil purpose.

"*Ah, hae, hae*"*!* he cried. "Oh, wretch that I am. Ah, the unluckiness of everything. Help! Help! good people. The Rani has been abducted."

In a few seconds guards ran with all haste to the spot; figures emerged from the tents, a babel of tongues rose above the wail of the secretary. Presently, to Bipin's surprise, the Rani herself appeared on the scene.

"What is all this"? she demanded. "Bipin art thou intoxicated, or has thy sleep been possessed by a nightmare"?

"Oh, great Lady," he cried. "Tell me, I implore thee, is it, in truth, thyself, who speakest"?

"To be sure," she replied. "Who else should it be. Thou art becoming a tiresome fellow," she added, "with thy midnight adventures. Disclose, what manner of creature hast thou been in combat with now"?

"Alas! great Rani," Bipin returned. "It was the terrible Ahmad Khan who compelled me to point out thy sleeping place, and he has gone off with I know not whom."

"Ahmad Khan"! the Rani exclaimed, as the truth of his design flashed upon her. "Now, by Heaven"! she cried angrily. "I will bear no more with him. Go," she commanded to the captain of her guard, "mount with a troop and follow swiftly. Thou art to bring him to me alive or dead. The beast hath gone mad and must be exterminated."

The officer obeyed her order with dispatch. He rode forth in the direction it was said Ahmad Khan had taken, but in the darkness soon lost the track. At daybreak he was forced to return with the intelligence that Ahmad had escaped.

Meanwhile Ahmad galloped northward with savage joy in his heart. He clasped the insensible captive form tightly in his arms.

"Now Allah be thanked," he muttered exultingly. "The fair Rani, the fickle beauty can escape me no longer."

He rode with all speed for a long distance in fear of pursuit, but at last he could restrain his impatient desire to gaze upon her face no longer.

The day was breaking as he halted his party. He moved a little apart, and uncovered the fold of linen over the woman's head. He directed his eyes with passionate rapture upon the unveiled face; then broke out into a volley of oaths.

"Hell's fiends," he shouted, as his astonished gaze beheld an old and wrinkled countenance. "What damnable trick of fortune is this? Am I bewitched"?

His arms mechanically released the figure of an aged servant of the Rani. She fell to the ground, and, recovering her senses, sat moaning pitifully.

For a time, Ahmad was too dumbfounded to take any

other course than to explode curse after curse. Then his mortification and fury burst upon the heads of the two attendants, who had been chief parties to the misadventure. He rode at them with uplifted sword, but they warily parried his blows, to finally disarm their master.

"What will my Lord do now"? they asked significantly.

Truly, what would Ahmad Khan do now? was the question. To return to the Rani's camp was impossible. There was no choice but to go forward.

"Get thee home, hag," he addressed the terrified woman, and bear Ahmad Khan's best *salaams* to thy noble mistress. Tell her, he hath grown weary of her court and her caprices."

With fury he drove his spurs into his horse's flanks. By night and day, with little rest, he rode for that lawless territory beyond the Afghan border. There, his own followers seized an opportunity to relieve him of his life and treasure.

In a barren, rocky pass, his body lay, pierced by a dozen wounds, exposed to the vulture and the lion; while his murderers, in retreat, quarrelled and fought over the price of their treachery.

It was a pitiless closing scene, in keeping with his nature.

Chapter XXV

FOR MY COUNTRY

GWALIOR was captured by the Rani of Jhansi. Such was the astounding news carried swiftly from end to end of the Indian Peninsula. The Natives, for the greater part, hailed it either with secret or open joy, many nobles, with their retainers, hastening to join the standard of the redoutable Princess. To the Foreigners, it brought astonishment and perplexity, with fears that the whole rebellion would burst forth anew. They realized that a second Jeanne D'Arc, as valiant in battle, more subtle in council than the Maid of Orleans, moved by the same passionate love for her country, had cast in their teeth a wager of defiance, to stand until either they were driven from her state, or she had perished.

It was no hour for deliberation. Her *coup de main* had been so well timed, that unless Gwalior was immediately recaptured, the rains would descend, making the country impassable for military operations, and her position thus secure for months to come. The result was unpleasant to conjecture.

With all haste the army of Central India, that had retired to quarters for the approaching season of storm, was reorganized, and the general who had fought against the Rani at Jhansi, at Kunch, and at Kalpi, marched forth to another test of skill. In his long and honorable career he had never met an opposing leader more worthy of his steel.

In the meantime the Rani threw all the force of her character, all the energy of both her body and mind, into preparations for the struggle she quickly perceived was at hand. She fully appreciated the material advantage she had gained, she also understood the weaknesses of her comrades in arms—their tendency to prolong the festivities in celebration of their victory, their unconquerable disposition to retreat the moment the Foreigners closed in battle. But now that she was in supreme command, she determined that at Gwalior it would either be another victory, or death for herself and the majority of her companions.

"Canst thou not rest for a little, dear Rani"? Prasad asked, when after days of untiring energy she continued to bend her efforts to perfect the defenses. "If the Foreigners come, surely we are safe from them here."

"Nay Prasad," she returned. "No rest will I take while danger threatens, and this work remains uncompleted. But in a little there will come a long rest for me, either in thy arms, my love; or in those of God."

Prasad, the Rao Sahib, even Tantia Topi, through his jealousy, marvelled at the spirit of the woman. They curtailed their feasting, and zealously furthered her commands.

The general belief that the Foreigners would not march upon Gwalior before the rains was soon dispelled. From two directions, the East and South, it was learned, that the enemy was rapidly approaching. It was evident they regarded the recapture of Gwalior as of supreme importance.

It was impossible for the Rani to superintend in person the long line of defenses raised before Gwalior, so she delegated the command of those to the south to Tantia Topi, reserving for herself the less strongly fortified position amid the hills and ravines to the south-east of the city, lying between that place and the village of Kotah-ki-sari. There she awaited the army advancing from the east, impatiently for a few days; with still greater impatience on the Sixteenth of June, when the distant roar of cannon announced that Tantia Topi was engaged with the Foreigners at Morar, on her extreme right.

Throughout the day various reports reached her ears. At one time, it was claimed, that the Foreigners were successively repulsed, beaten, and in full retreat; later, that Tantia Topi was as usual practicing masterly tactics in a retrograde movement.

"Ah, now, may God curse his cowardice," she cried passionately, to the messenger. "Return with all speed and order him to stand wherever he may be; for if I find him in the Gwalior fortress, one of us shall die for it."

But Tantia was not of standing fibre before Foreign bayonets. If in little else, he was a genius in limbering up his guns and dragging them away from desperate positions. That night the Rani was informed that he had succeeded in executing a clever strategic act. He had held the Foreigners at bay until he was able to move back upon Gwalior in good order with his guns, abandoning Morar, a useless place, to the enemy. On the morrow he believed he would rout them utterly.

The Rani's anger, her contempt for such conduct of warfare, could scarcely find expression in words or action. She sat in her tent, sick at heart, pondering deeply over the situation.

"What can I do"? she murmured. "I cannot command at all points of this wide field at the same moment. Is there no one but me who hath the courage to dash forward? These Foreigners are only men like ourselves. They are not Gods. God knows, far from it. Have I not seen many of them perish at Jhansi, at Kunch, and at Kalpi"?

"Go," she commanded to an aid-de-camp. "Go to Tantia Topi, and say that if he doth make such another masterly retreat, the Rani of Jhansi will aid herself by attacking him in rear, and driving him on to the enemy's bayonets."

Then she retired to a temple and prayed long and fervently to the God of Battles, that on the morrow her troops might be endowed with invincible courage, that once more He would give her arms a victory.

The day broke with an atmosphere charged with sweltering heat. Soon the rocks and sand burned to the touch as if but a thin crust lay between their feet and a mighty furnace. If its oppressiveness was felt by the Rani's troops, it bore tenfold more heavily upon the Foreigners, fatigued by a long march.

The Rani had taken up a position with cavalry, artillery and infantry among the hills intervening between the enemy and the plain of Gwalior. Her plan was to draw the Foreigners into the ravines by a feint of retreat, holding them there in conflict with intrenched infantry and masked batteries, while she swept down with her cavalry through a flank defile upon their rear. She might thus capture their baggage and ammunition train, throwing their front into hopeless confusion.

At daybreak she beheld the enemy advance to the assault.

All through that day the battle was waged with desperate valor on both sides. Step by step the Foreigners fought their way into the ravines, driving the Native troops before them. At different stages the Rani rode into the thick of the combat to animate her followers, with Prasad bearing her standard. Her counter attack was delivered at an opportune moment, but was frustrated. Evening approached to find both armies exhausted, the Rani's first position captured, but her forces still held well together. A decisive victory could not as yet be claimed by either side; for the Rani had decided to continue the battle throughout the night.

It was in a moment of temporary rest, that the Foreign general ordered his cavalry to charge, with the object of driving the Rani's bodyguard out into the Gwalior plain. The movement took the latter by surprise, with a resulting panic.

The Rani bravely fronted the oncoming squadrons in an endeavor to rally her troopers, but in the tumult her horse took the bit in its teeth and carried her away in the rout. At their heels the Foreign horsemen were slashing and firing their pistols mercilessly. Again and again the Rani called on her troopers to halt, but they only rode for the camp the faster. She reined in her horse and turned, to find she was the last on that part of the field. A hussar was upon her with uplifted sword.

The blow fell but she parried it adroitly, and delivered another in return that slightly wounded her assailant. More hussars coming fast in their leader's wake, the odds were too uneven against her. She set her horse at a ditch a few yards in front, beyond which was safety. The brute urged by her voice leaped forward to the bank, then refused to jump, stumbled and fell with its rider. Before she could extricate herself, the hussar dashed upon her with fury nettled by the pain of his wound. As he swept by, he leveled his pistol and fired. The bullet lodged in her breast, her sword fell from her hand, she sank to the ground in unconsciousness to rise no more.

Over the ditch the hussar passed little thinking that he had dealt a mortal wound to the "bravest and best" of the Native leaders. In his eyes she had appeared only as one of their officers.

Soon the Foreigners' bugles sounded the recall, the Rani's bodyguard rallied and charged back over the field, but it was too late to save their mistress. They discovered her where she had fallen, and gently, sadly, bore her back to her tent.

There it was made apparent that her end was quickly approaching. Prasad, heartbroken, bitterly reproached himself that he had not remained at her side to protect her from harm. He had taken her lifeless form in his arms. About them were grouped men who had never before experienced a tender emotion. Tears coursed down their fierce, bronzed, visages.

Prasad's gentle caresses at last recalled the Rani to consciousness.

"Well Prasad," she asked in a faint voice. "How went the battle? All is not lost I hope, though I am wounded to the death."

"Ah, dear one," he sadly returned. "All is truly lost with thee."

"Do not speak thus," she replied, painfully exerting herself to a return of spirit. "While brave men live no cause is lost."

Then turning her gaze upon the grief stricken countenances of her troopers, she enjoined them not to weep for her.

"For thy tears will bring forth mine," she pleaded, "and the true soldier cries not on facing death."

With assistance, she then removed Sindhia's necklace from her breast. She directed the strings to be broken, and summoning her ever faithful Valaitis gave to each, in turn, a pearl in remembrance of their fair captain.

"Farewell," she said, as each saluted with uncontrolled grief. "Be brave and fight on until the end."

Soon Prasad remained with her alone.

For a time she rested her head upon his breast with her arms about him. Many loving, sorrowful words were exchanged, until she felt the moment of dissolution nigh.

"Prasad," she said. "Place thy hand within my jacket. Thou wilt find my parting gift to thee there."

He obeyed as she directed, and drew forth his dagger.

"Thy dagger, O Prasad," she exclaimed. "I have kept it to protect my honor. I give it back to thee to save thine own in case of need. And now, my dear Lord, one request have I to ask of thee before I say farewell. I beg thou wilt see to it, that no Foreign eye doth gaze upon my body after I am dead."

In a sorrowful whisper he promised to comply.

"Then farewell," she said. "Farewell Prasad, may God love thee as truly as I have done."

"Farewell"? he exclaimed interrogatively. "I will not leave thee yet alone."

"Prasad," she returned. "It is my will to be alone. Nay, I shall not be alone. Again I say, farewell to thee, for thine eyes must not behold my last moment."

He embraced her once more, laid her gently back amid the pillows, then rose obediently to her command. He paused on the threshold of the entrance to gaze for the last time upon her face. In its beautiful features there was discernible neither sign of weakness nor of fear—her spirit remained heroic to the end. He covered his eyes with his hands and passed forth.

Within the tent a profound, mysterious, silence fell, as the darkness of night descended on the land. The Rani clapsed her hands upon her breast as her lips murmured a last prayer.

"Great God of Gods. O most holy, omnipotent One. If I have sinned against the laws of my caste, it was for the love of my country. Surely thou wilt forgive a woman who has tried to inspire others to be brave and just. O India," she cried, raising herself with difficulty upon her side and stretching forth her arms, "farewell. Farewell my people, my brave soldiers whom I have loved to lead in battle against the foe. Not forever shall their horsemen ride triumphantly through the land. A day will come when their law shall be no longer obeyed, and our temples and palaces rise anew from their ruins. Farewell! Farewell! O Gods of my fathers, be with me now."

She drew the folds of a shawl over her face to hide her death agony, and again lay down. The blackness of night grew deeper, the silence more intense. Presently, strange, warrior forms seemed to appear from the unknown and filled the Rani's tent. One supremely beautiful figure, in dazzling raiment, came forth to enfold the dying woman in her arms.

In a little, a wail of lamentation rose across the intervening space between the camps of the two armies. The Foreign soldiers asked its meaning of one another.

The answer might have been, that the spirit of the heroic Lachmi Bai had been gathered to the protecting arms of Param-eswara, the merciful, the just, the all supreme God, alike of the Hindu, the Mohammedan, and the Christian.

The Rani of Jhansi was dead.

* * * * * * * *

Great was the pomp and solemn the ceremony with which they carried out her last desire, so that even her body might not fall into the hands of the enemy.

Before the day had come again, a long procession took its way from Sindhia's palace to a point on the bank of the Morar river, where a flower-decked funeral pyre had been erected.

In the van troopers marched with mournful step, followed by officers bearing torches. Then came Brahman priests, naked to the waist in performance of their sacred office. They chanted from the Vedas and scattered rice upon the way. These preceded the bier, upon which, under a canopy of cloth of gold, lay the body of the Rani, attired in royal robes, with the marks of her high caste set upon her forehead. Directly following, walked her aged *guru,* whose solemn duty it would be, in the absence of a relative, to ignite the funeral pyre. Lastly, Prasad with the Rao Sahib, attended by all the nobles of the court.

Beside the whole length of the route traversed by the procession, a multitude of people had gathered, whose lamentations rent the air.

The bier was carried slowly to its destination, and seven times round the funeral pyre. Then the Rani's body was lifted tenderly and placed upon its last bed of death, rice was scattered over all, and the dry brush, saturated with *ghee,* ignited.

The flames leaped high, illuminating many weeping faces, and throwing into relief the figures of Brahmans, nobles, and officers, grouped in a majestic scene. Quickly the tongues of fire reduced to ashes the Rani's mortal form. These, the priests reverentially collected, and, with prayers, cast them upon the waters of the river, to be carried into the bosom of holy Ganges.

"Farewell," cried Prasad, as he stood upon the bank. "Farewell, thou brave, dear Rani. I doubt not I shall be with thee soon."

That day the sun of India hid its face behind gathering clouds, the storm, the monsoon burst.

THE END